Christian A. Schwarz
THE 3 COLORS OF LOVE

If it is true that any book has numerous authors (in the sense that multiple individuals contribute to its contents, layout, and style), it is especially true for **The 3 Colors of Love.**

First of all, there are **those who participated in my conferences** and seminars, with whom I was able to field-test the concepts and whose positive and negative feedback shapes almost every single page of this book. In the context of these events, I learned immeasurably more than I was able to give—not only for the writing of this book, but also for my own ability to love. Thank you.

Throughout my travels, I have continually discussed the concepts behind this book with our **NCD National Partners** and their teams on all six continents. I have learned much more from them than I could ever have learned through academic studies—especially in terms of distinguishing between the universal principles of the gospel and my own "culturally flavored" preferences. Their creative input has made this book a truly multi-cultural project. Thank you.

As with previous NCD books, my friend and colleague **Christoph Schalk** and his team have taken great care to work on the normation of the test materials. Since I know the value of a scientifically-developed test as opposed to a "home made version," I am extremely grateful for this contribution of both intellectual excellence and personal commitment. Thank you.

When writing in a language that is not your native tongue, you learn how dependent you are on the assistance of other people. One of the greatest privileges of my ministry is the cooperation of **Jon and Kathy Haley**, who originally started as my English editors, but have now become core participants in the creative team for the NCD tools. Thank you.

It is almost an authorial ritual to close one's acknowledgements by saying thank you to one's spouse, usually for the long hours of doing without their partner when he or she has been busy writing. What a gift that you are so different, **Brigitte**: You have constantly persuaded me, motivated me, even pushed me to spend more time in my office in order to see this book come together. You have made it possible for family and ministry, management and friendship, business and prayer to come together in our home as a beautiful symphony. In you I can truly see all three colors of God's love at work. Thank you, Brigitte.

Christian A. Schwarz

# The 3 Colors of Love

### The art
### of giving and receiving
### justice, truth, and grace

NCD DISCIPLESHIP RESOURCES

**ChurchSmart**
RESOURCES

# 10 distinctives
# of this series

There are many excellent books on discipleship, Christian ministry, and church development. What then are the distinctives of the **NCD Discipleship Resources**? Natural Church Development (NCD) is a new approach to church growth, the foundations of which are described in the books *Natural Church Development, The Threefold Art of Experiencing God* and *Paradigm Shift in the Church.* All of the books in this series are...

**1. trinitarian:** Since God has revealed himself in a threefold way—as Creator, in Jesus, and in the Holy Spirit—we can experience him in three different ways. The three colors—green for the "creation revelation," red for the "salvation revelation," and blue for the "personal revelation"—are central symbols in all of the **NCD Discipleship Resources**. The books draw practical applications from God's major acts in history: Creation, Calvary, and Pentecost.

**2. natural:** Natural Church Development builds on the biblical insight that good roots inevitably produce good fruit. If the quality of church life is high, a church will grow quantitatively. Therefore, **NCD Discipleship Resources** focus primarily on the "roots." Our task is not to "make" a church grow, but rather to release the growth potential that God has already implanted. Then the church will grow "all by itself."

**3. church centered:** **NCD Discipleship Resources** are designed in such a way that they can be used by individual believers, Christian groups and whole churches. The quality of a church is determined by the quality of its people and their interpersonal and ministry relationships. Therefore, it is characteristic of this series that "discipleship" is understood in a broader sense than in traditional usage, and the books help implement this kind of integrated discipleship.

**4. research based:** NCD is based on comprehensive research conducted by the Institute for Natural Church Development in Germany. At this point, more than 30,000 churches in about 60 countries on all continents have participated in the study. The goal of this research has been to identify universal church growth principles. All of the concepts described in the **NCD Discipleship Resources** are based on insights derived from these studies.

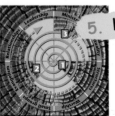

**5. holistic:** Each of the **NCD Discipleship Resources** covers one of the eight "quality characteristics" of Natural Church Development. Rather than stressing one element as a "universal key," the goal of NCD is to bring together all eight elements holistically. With the help of the NCD Survey, any church can easily identify which of these quality characteristics require special attention.

### 6. creative:

**NCD Discipleship Resources** do not impose a specific model on other Christians: "Do it my way, and your church will grow." Instead, they try to stimulate individuality, spontaneity, and creativity. The series is based on the fact that every believer is unique and has his or her particular divine gifting. The same holds true for churches. The goal of NCD is to nurture this God-given uniqueness.

### 7. international:

NCD has built a network with National Partners in about 60 countries. This has enabled truly global learning processes to take place. Rather than communicating the specifics of one culture to another, the goal of this endeavor has been to collect the most helpful concepts from all six continents and to present them in such a way that they can be used internationally. **NCD Discipleship Resources** are available in multiple languages.

### 8. colorful:

God has made all of life colorful. Since **NCD Discipleship Resources** are designed to communicate these colors, they cannot communicate them in black and white. Therefore, all books in this series are in full color. However, since the discipleship series is produced as an international co-production in many different language versions, it can be offered for the price of ordinary black-and-white books.

### 9. biblical:

**NCD Discipleship Resources** are biblical, but they are not designed as "Bible-study books." NCD holds the Bible as the normative standard. Everything that can be learned from other churches, from research, or from nature, is evaluated in light of biblical principles. Only those concepts that pass this test have been incorporated into this series. Its primary goal is to show the relevance of the Word of God to our daily lives.

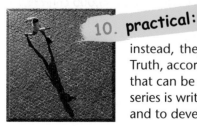

### 10. practical:

**NCD Discipleship Resources** are not focused on increasing mere intellectual knowledge; instead, they seek to assist in the practical application of knowledge. Truth, according to the Bible, is not an abstract concept, but something that can be discovered by "doing it." Thus, every single chapter in this series is written to help you discover practical ways to serve God better and to develop a healthy, relevant, and attractive church.

**NCD DISCIPLESHIP RESOURCES**

# A different approach
# ... for different results

*The 3 Colors of Love* is one of the eight books that will be published in the *NCD Discipleship Resources* series. Each book will cover one of the eight quality characteristics of growing churches.

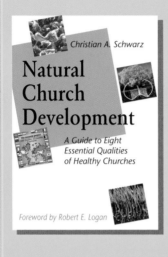

The foundational introduction to Natural Church Development:

Christian A. Schwarz
**Natural Church Development**
Hardcover, 128 pages, fully illustrated, with over 100 full-color photos and graphics
ISBN 1-889638-00-5
Retail price $20.00 in U.S. dollars

Working material related to the theory and practice of Natural Church Development is available in about 40 languages. Titles and ordering information can be found on the internet at:

***www.ncd-international.org***
***www.ChurchSmart.com***

*Retail price $10.00 – Quantity discounts available*
*Call 1-800-253-4276 for current pricing*

*Published by ChurchSmart Resources*
*St. Charles, IL 60174*

© 2004 by Christian A. Schwarz
C & P Verlag, Emmelsbüll, Germany

© U.S.A. edition: 2004 by ChurchSmart Resources
3830 Ohio Ave., St. Charles, IL 60174

Edited by Jon & Kathy Haley

Scripture taken from *Holy Bible: New International Version*®
© 1973, 1978, 1984 by International Bible Society. Used by permission of Zondervan Publishing House. All rights reserved.

Layout and artwork by Christian A. Schwarz

Printing: M.C.E. HOREB, Viladecavalls (Barcelona) – Printed in Spain

*Photocopying not allowed. All rights reserved.*

ISBN 1-889638-45-5

# The 3 Colors of Love

**Introduction:**
Reflecting all the colors of God's love     9

**Chapter 1:**
**What are the three colors of love?     11**
The hunger for love     12
The love deficiencies in our churches     14
Misconceptions of love     16
God is love     18
Three dimensions of God's love     20
God is light     23
What is darkness?     26
Practicing love means reflecting God's light     28
The color green: justice     30
The color red: truth     32
The color blue: grace     34
Three models of love in action     36
Model for justice: James     37
Model for truth: John     38
Model for grace: Paul     39
What does this mean in practice?     40
Primary and secondary virtues     41
Strengths and liabilities of different cultures     44
Two approaches in conflict     46
Love can be learned     48
Your personal growth process     50

**Chapter 2:**
**How to reflect God's love     53**
Fruit is visible     54
Understanding the fruit of the Spirit     56
1 Corinthians 13 and the spiritual color wheel     60
The Fruit of the Spirit Test     62
How to evaluate the Fruit of the Spirit Test     67
Which color area do you have to address?     69
What do the individual terms mean?     70
The fruit of patience: Enduring love     71
The fruit of joy: Rejoicing love     72
The fruit of peace: Reconciling love     73
The fruit of faithfulness: Reliable love     74
The fruit of goodness: Correcting love     75
The fruit of kindness: Amiable love     76
The fruit of self-control: Disciplined love     77
The fruit of gentleness: Humble love     78
Love is indivisible     79

**Chapter 3:**
**Twelve exercises that can**
**revolutionize your life    81**
Exercise 1: Fill up with God's love    82
Exercise 2: Love yourself    85
Exercise 3: Wear other people's glasses    87
Exercise 4: Put an end to spiritual hypocrisy    91
Exercise 5: Learn to trust    94
Exercise 6: Make yourself vulnerable    97
Exercise 7: Dare to forgive    100
Exercise 8: Be transparent    103
Exercise 9: Train active listening    107
Exercise 10: Surprise with gifts    110
Exercise 11: Use your humor    112
Exercise 12: Have a meal together    115

**Chapter 4:**
**Eight exercises to transform your church**
**into an oasis of love    117**
Exercise 1: "Give off your scent, gentlemen!"    118
Exercise 2: "Just for the fun of it"    120
Exercise 3: "Boredom forbidden"    123
Exercise 4: "Glad you're here"    126
Exercise 5: "Let me walk in your moccasins"    128
Exercise 6: "The oikos principle"    131
Exercise 7: "What are your spiritual gifts?"    134
Exercise 8: "May I pray for you?"    138

**Epilogue:**
**The greatest power on planet earth    140**

**NCD Implementation Resources:**
**The "how to" series    143**

**NCD Discipleship Resources:**
**The "3-Color" series    144**

# Reflecting all the colors of God's love

I remember the scene in all of its revealing comedy as if it had happened yesterday. I had been invited to share the initial results of our research of more than 1000 churches worldwide with a group of church growth experts. Since I had only twenty minutes for my presentation, I decided to focus on *one* example of our findings that I believed was representative of the whole project. "In growing churches," I said, "there is measurably more laughter than in non-growing ones. This is one of the most provable church growth principles I know."

The reaction of the experts? The group broke into laughter. "Very funny, Christian. Ha ha ha. All of us like your sense of humor. But you certainly don't expect us to believe that you have invested several years of your life just to come up with stories like this. Please, tell us the hard facts of your research, the strategically relevant points." I replied, "Gentlemen, these *are* the hard facts. These *are* the very factors that are strategically relevant in order to win the world for Christ."

> When you choose to grow in love, you are not dealing with a weekend hobby, but with the heart of the Christian faith.

The laughter dissipated, but only to be substituted by clear signs of disappointment. Some of those present pointedly checked their wrist watches, leaving it to me to decide whether this was a sign of protest or sheer boredom. The rest of the afternoon they continued to focus on those items that *they* believed were most relevant to church growth: management methods, marketing tools, leadership techniques, famous church models.

### Why laughter is a symptom of health

Why did I choose to put "laughter," of all things, at the center of my presentation? Once we realize what kind of church life is needed to create an "upbeat" atmosphere, it becomes clear why laughter in the church is a sign of health. In a healthy church, people are able to laugh at themselves. They know they are forgiven. They know they are accepted. Salvation has touched their whole being, not just their brains. Authentic joy is shared, personally and publicly. Yes, it is fun to be part of such a church.

It is *this* kind of atmosphere that we need to facilitate, model, radiate, teach, and learn; it is the atmosphere of love. That is the reason why this book is included as one of eight building blocks in the *NCD Discipleship Resources* series.

### Three distinctives of this book

In the development of this tool, I have read more than 200 books on loving relationships. Many of them are excellent. What, then, are the distinctives of the book you hold in your hands?

1. Believe it or not, even the majority of Christian books on this subject are based more on a secular-romantic notion of love than on a biblical understanding. Since the biblical concept is far superior to

any other concept, I have placed it at the center of this book. As with all of the other tools in this series, *The 3 Colors of Love* is based on a **trinitarian ("three color") compass** that is at the strategic root of Natural Church Development (NCD). While trinitarian teaching, as many of us have experienced it, tends to be irrelevant for our daily lives, in NCD, the trinitarian compass has proven to be one of the most practical tools imaginable, with revolutionary consequences for what we will be doing next Monday, Tuesday, Wednesday and the rest of the week. You will experience it!

2. One of the most visible consequences of our approach is that it doesn't treat everyone alike. It has been very frustrating for me to discover that many books on loving relationships do just that. All of a sudden, *all of us* have to pay more attention to our feelings ... or learn how to confront ... or focus on social justice. Nonsense! While some readers may truly need to work on one of these areas, others might have to stress different aspects in order to grow in love. Depending on our **individual starting points**, we may have to follow very different paths in order to reflect God's love more fully.

> It has been very frustrating to discover that many tools treat everyone alike.

3. As you will quickly see and hopefully appreciate, this book originated in the context of **cross-cultural ministry**. This has shaped the theoretical paradigm on which the practical exercises are built. I have learned that a number of Oriental cultures (in several Asian and Arab countries) seem to be, in many respects, closer to the original biblical concepts than Western societies. Numerous misunderstandings about love result from the fact that many cultures—especially those with a Greek/Indo-European heritage—have drifted far away from the Oriental roots of their Christian faith. It is beneficial for all cultures to learn from others. This is what globalization is—or should I say: ought to be?—all about.

### Love—the center of the Christian faith

When you choose to grow in love, you are not dealing with a weekend hobby that may be of interest to you, but others can safely ignore. You are dealing with the heart of the Christian faith. At the same time you are dealing with the heart of church development. The *motive* of church development is love, the *message* is love, and it is empirically demonstrable that there is no better church growth *method* than love.

It is my prayer that believers who work through this book will become increasingly open channels for the love of God, being able to reflect all the colors of God's love more fully than they do now. This will create a natural growth dynamic in our churches that is much more powerful than all of the clever marketing techniques in the world. Get ready to see it happen!

*Christian A. Schwarz*          *Institute for Natural Church Development*

# What are the three colors of love?

*Love. It is one of the most central words of Christian theology, and yet one of the foggiest words on planet earth. Many Christians who use this term communicate a clearly secular understanding rather than a fully biblical concept. Sometimes it almost seems that as Christians we haven't even really begun to grasp the full scope of the biblical concept of love, let alone put it into practice. But what is the biblical understanding of love?*

Chapter 1:
Foundations

# The hunger for love

I t was at a seminar in Switzerland... I had spent the whole day with an extraordinarily motivated group, discussing a number of key issues: What are the vital signs of growing churches? How can we involve more people in ministry? How can we enable the groups in our churches to multiply? I was in my element, sharing my insights with the use of diagrams, questionnaires, and statistics.

> "I attend a famous, growing church— and yet I feel like I'm the loneliest person on planet earth."

At the end of the evening, as I was just gathering my scattered overhead sheets for the next day, a woman approached me. "I don't doubt that you're right in every single point you have made," she said. I thanked her for the compliment.

She continued, "But I found it difficult to even listen to you. Everything just flew past me as if it had nothing whatsoever to do with me." Another case of someone fleeing responsibility, I thought. "And why do you think church development has nothing to do with you?" I asked, my eyes and mind still focused on the transparencies.

She started to talk. She told me how deeply she had been hurt by the disagreements in her church over the past few years ... how her small group had broken up as a result ... how some of her best friends had been avoiding her ... how her husband, who had never shared her church involvement, had recently left her ... how other church members hardly ever had time for her because they were so occupied with all sorts of church growth activities ... how she had repeatedly offered to take over responsibilities in the church, but her offers had always been declined. "Sort out your family problems first," she had been told.

"I attend a famous, growing church," she said, "and yet I feel like I'm the loneliest person on planet earth." As she said this, tears came to her eyes.

## A paradigm shift

It's embarrassing for me to tell you the rest of the story, but perhaps you can learn from my lack of sensitivity. I told this woman that I was terribly sorry about her situation, but unfortunately it was not my field of expertise. My specialty was church growth. I advised her to find a Christian counselor to help her with her problems. She then went home, and I went to my hotel room.

That night, however, I couldn't sleep. I wasn't able to get this woman's face out of my mind. The more I thought about our conversation, the less I was able to forgive myself for brushing her off so brusquely. Sure, my field is church growth. But what is church growth all about? More programs? More groups? More activities? More "busyness"? For heaven's sake, that cannot be the future of our churches! All of the church growth programs in the world should be trucked to the town dump if they don't help to create a place where lonely, hurting people like this woman can find comfort, support, and healing. The next morning, that woman did not attend the seminar. I haven't heard from her since.

Why do I share this experience with you? Because it was this woman who caused a paradigm shift in my ministry. I have discovered that our churches are full of people like her—lonely, hurt, and disappointed. I even believe that every one of us, in one way or another, suffers from similar feelings. Only a few believers are in a group where there is enough trust for them to be able to open up their hearts and experience the healing power of God's love through other people.

### The primary problem: lack of love

Some time ago, I asked the participants of a Natural Church Development seminar to write on a piece of paper what they thought were the greatest barriers to church growth. One person wrote, "fights." Someone else wrote, "power struggles." Others wrote, "rumors," "indifference," "overworked leadership," "traditionalism," "stubbornness," "narrow-mindedness," "lack of trust." I suggested that all of these barriers could be summarized in three words: "lack of love." Almost every head nodded in agreement.

Lack of love. In spite of the dominance of this theme in the media, that is *the* illness of our times. Pop lyrics and cheap romance novels are no more than an expression of this common disorder. Hardly any subject is emphasized as much as love. And yet ...

> What use are the best church growth programs in the world if they don't help to create a place where lonely, hurting people can find comfort, support, and healing?

- Loneliness will soon be the most widespread malady in Western societies, though it is definitely not limited only to them. Recent surveys show that a quarter of the populace suffers from chronic loneliness. It is one of the major causes of suicide.

- In some countries, about one of every two marriages ends in divorce. Most people long for a harmonious relationship. But in the United States alone, one marriage breaks down every minute—24 hours a day.

- The number of mental illnesses has reached shocking proportions in recent years. Every fifth patient who consults a general practitioner suffers from either a mental disorder or physical symptom resulting from mental causes. Leading psychiatrists tell us that a lack of love is the main cause of serious neurotic disorders.

These statistics, sad as they are, do not reveal the full extent of the suffering experienced in our society. They cannot express what it really means to have an unfulfilled hunger for love. Where are the churches that can satisfy this hunger? Where are the Christians who reflect God's love in such a way that God's healing power can be experienced in our world?

# The love deficiencies in our churches

I t is too easy to resort to cheap caricatures of the world's distorted concept of love, as is frequently done in some sermons: "Brothers and sisters, just look at the world outside. People who live without God are caught in a prison of self-centeredness, inevitably understanding love as a hidden form of egotism. But the Christian knows ..." And the sermon goes on to describe in the most beautiful terms the wonderful reality of the love found in Christian churches.

This kind of teaching makes me feel very uncomfortable. It's certainly not completely unjustified to criticize the secular concept of love (we will constantly do it in this book). However, before we Christians criticize "the world's false concept of love," we would do well to consider carefully how loving our churches and groups really are ... and how accurate our own concept of love is.

### "Christian" hindrances to love

*Before we Christians criticize "the world's false concept of love," we would do well to consider how loving our churches are.*

In other words, we should not only criticize those who confuse love with sexual greed and make a profit from it. Rather, we should also focus on those ...

... who muddle along so monotonously in their churches and groups that no one ever experiences Christian love in action, even if they use the term till they're blue in the face;

... who sit next to each other in the worship service Sunday after Sunday, but never get to know each other beyond the "How are you?" level;

... who are involved in many activities within the church, but do nothing to help nonbelievers find a personal relationship with Jesus and thus experience the love of God;

... who are tireless evangelists, but use the "battering ram" method rather than radiating the love of God;

... who fight aggressively against devotional styles and traditions that differ from their own (of course, just for the sake of "purity" in the kingdom of God);

... who build barriers around their churches that prove to be far more difficult for outsiders to overcome than the Berlin Wall;

... who suffocate others in an oppressive church environment, rather than enabling them to breath the liberating air of love.

### Loving and unloving churches

Over the past few years, I have had the privilege of getting to know hundreds of churches on all six continents, many of them being wonderful examples of Christian love in action. They not only meet the needs of their members, but also reach out to their communities in very creative ways. I have gained many of the insights shared in this book from these churches.

The sad thing, however, is that I have also encountered the very opposite kind of churches: communities in which believers may grow in their knowledge of the Bible, but not in their ability to love. It would be misleading to see these churches as "exceptions to the rule." Unfortunately, this type of church seems to be more prevalent than the positive type. These churches are literally frozen, and upon joining such a congregation you're in danger of catching emotional hypothermia. Their doctrine might be correct, but they give off a negative energy that is almost physically palpable.

### "Touching forbidden"

Years ago, my wife and I had to travel by train through Germany. In Cologne, we had a one hour layover. Since the Cologne Cathedral is located directly across from the train station and I had never been inside of it before, we decided to take a quick spin through the cathedral. I must admit that I had certain spiritual expectations about visiting this church. Some of my friends had told me, "Christian, the moment you enter that cathedral you sense the presence of God."

> "In the church, one doesn't wish to see people embracing each other."

It was a wonderfully bright and sunny day when Brigitte and I climbed the stairs to the cathedral. As soon as we passed through the door, all of that brilliant light disappeared. The massive architecture and the dark atmosphere of the church gave me an instant sense of fear. I subconsciously did what probably most of us would do in such a state—I placed my arm around Brigitte's shoulder and moved closer to her, in search of at least a little bit of warmth in that unwelcoming environment. No sooner had my arm touched Brigitte's shoulder, when one of the monks ministering in the cathedral approached us. "Sir, put your arm down immediately," he said. "In the church, one doesn't wish to see people embracing each other." He then asked us to give an offering for the upkeep of the cathedral...

Brigitte and I left the church as quickly as possible. The last few yards, we were running. We pushed through the doors into the bright and sunny day. There were street musicians singing. People were laughing. It was warm. We could breath. We felt relieved. We felt closer to God.

### A symbol for many churches

For me, this experience has become symbolic of the situation in numerous churches. In spite of all of the good things that can be said about them—and I have no doubt that there are many wonderful things that could be said about the Cologne Cathedral, or at least its architecture—for many people they communicate the very opposite of what Christian love is all about. But doesn't the Bible tell us that love should be the very sign by which Christians can be identified (John 13:35)?

# Misconceptions of love

How is it possible for a church to be so underdeveloped in its ability to love that it actually cultivates the very disease it was originally intended to cure? It can be demonstrated that vast segments of the Christian church have been massively influenced by misconceptions of love. Consequently, people firmly believe that their personal understanding of love is exactly what the Bible teaches. In reality, they have become so accustomed to false concepts that they read them into the Bible. Whenever they see "love" in Scripture, they perceive it as a confirmation of their previously shaped view. For most of us, the term "love" is so strongly associated with certain inner images that whenever we come across the word, those images automatically surface. It is not an exaggeration to say that Hollywood has had a stronger influence on our understanding of love than has the creator of heaven and earth, God Almighty.

*According to the secular-romantic notion, love is always soft, friendly, nice, and sentimental—the inner movies with roses and violins emerge.*

There are two particular misconceptions of love that I have often encountered in churches.

### Misconception no. 1: "Love is always soft"

This has become the standard understanding of love in everyday usage. This misconception, when translated to the Christian context, reduces "love" to a truncated version of "grace." It is certainly true, as we will see later, that grace is an integral part of love, but love cannot be reduced to grace alone. Grace is grace and love is love—two different terms, for good reasons. All that is characteristic of grace is covered by love; but grace doesn't cover all aspects of love. According to the secular-romantic notion, however, "tough" love, such as confronting people with the truth, is unimaginable. Love is always friendly, nice, and sentimental (the inner movies with roses and violins emerge). The end product is an exclusively soft (and sometimes alarmingly harmless) friendliness that no longer communicates real love, since it declines to help people fight sin and error in their lives.

Every believer knows that the Christian life isn't just about being nice and friendly and tender. In Scripture we read about truth, about justice, about hard measures in order to help people mature. But we also read that God is loving; even that he *is* love. How do we bring these two messages together?

The most frequent solution that I have encountered is this. We continue to use the term "love," but only in reference to its soft and friendly side. Then we go on: "God is love, to be sure, *but he is also just.*" Or: "We have to minister to people in love, *but also in truth.*" The term that has to be criticized in these sentences is not "love," or "justice," or "truth." What has to be criticized, from a biblical point of view, is the word "but." It suggests that "justice" and "truth" are almost the opposite of love—an understanding that is biblically untenable. Love is the very nature of God. Just as "grace" is an indispensable aspect of love, so also are "truth" and "justice." Truth and grace can be, at times, in tension with one other, but that is never the case with truth and love. Love that bypasses truth would no longer be love. That would be diametrically opposed to Paul's statement that love rejoices in the truth (1 Cor. 13:6).

### Misconception no. 2: "If you really love me, you must be an enemy of my enemies"

The second misconception begins at the other end of the spectrum. It is frequently found in groups that stress values such as "truth" or "justice." It's normal to find believers whose views, traditions, or practices are far removed from ours. It's also normal (or at least unavoidable) to perceive some of those individuals as "opponents." But what cannot be accepted is the idea that, in order to prove our love for them, some Christians insist that we must adopt all of their enemies. Having fellowship with them inevitably includes being part of their crusades against other believers.

Why is it that some churches cultivate the very diseases that they were intended to cure?

Let me illustrate. Our ministry is deliberately inter-denominational. I work with churches from various denominational backgrounds and different liturgical styles. I can sincerely say that I love these different Christian groups with all my heart, and that I am eager to support each one with all the creativity and resources at my disposal. But repeatedly I find that some of those I work with demand, "If you really want to be in fellowship with us, you should publicly separate yourself from XYZ."

For instance, I work with charismatic churches with the same enthusiasm as I work with those that are skeptical about them. Some of my charismatic friends doubt the seriousness of my love for them because I spend so much time with non-charismatic groups, whereas some of the non-charismatic churches feel that I am taking a position against them by co-operating with charismatic churches. To put it bluntly: For some I am a "heretic" because I shake hands with people that they regard as "heretics."

The underlying assumption is always the same: "If you really love me, you must be an enemy of my enemies." This thinking is so widespread among Christians that I regard it as one of the main hindrances to world evangelization. I am not suggesting that these groups stop trying to be advocates of the truth, but that in their paradigm one of the most important aspects of divine love is missing: the power to turn enemies into friends. Many of the groups I have encountered do just the opposite: they turn (potential) friends into enemies.

# God is love

I n John's first letter, we find a statement that was a totally new concept in the history of religion: "God is love" (1 John 4:8 and 16). The uniqueness of this concept becomes clear the moment we try to apply it to the deities of non-biblical religions: Manitou is love, Zeus, Jupiter, Brahma is love. These descriptions just wouldn't make any sense.

The truth that God is love is not only central to understanding the nature of God, but also to understanding the essence of love. It does not present love as merely one of God's characteristics ("God is *loving*"), rather it says, "God is *love*" (which means that love is the very nature of God). Since love is God's nature John could also say, "Whoever lives in love lives in God, and God in him" (1 John 4:16).

**We can only know what love is all about if we study how God dealt with people throughout the Bible.**

### God's characteristics and God's nature

When reading these verses superficially, many people tend to miss the significant difference between a "loving God" and a "God who is love." Actually, this is far more than just a difference in grammar or semantics. As we will see later, this distinction has dramatic consequences when it comes to practical ways of putting Christian love into action.

Note that the Bible never says that "God is justice" or "God is power" or "God is wisdom" or "God is anger." Certainly, it clearly speaks about God's justice, power, wisdom, and, especially in the New Testament, about his anger. But all of these are just *characteristics* of God that must not be confused with his *nature*. God loves justice, he reveals his power, he governs the world through wisdom, he demonstrates his anger. But he *is* love. Love is not just one of many traits in God's character that alternately move into the foreground or the background. God's nature is love. From there, his justice, his power, and his wisdom flows. Yes, even his anger flows from his love, and from nothing else.

### How do we define love?

God is love—this means that we can only know what love is all about if we know God, if we study how he dealt with people throughout the Bible. However, as we have already seen, most of us tend to arrive at our understanding of God from the opposite direction. The sequence is this:

1. We begin with our particular understanding of what love means (in most cases, shaped by the secular-romantic notion).

2. Then we read that "God is love."

3. Consequently, we project our secular-romantic notion on God.

In other words, we define "God" in terms of our own previously-conceived concept of love. What we should do, however, is define love in terms of what the Bible teaches us about the nature of God.

### The danger of projection

By following the first approach, which most of us tend to do, we end up with two false concepts:

- Our *concept of love* remains secular-romantic (since it was never evaluated in terms of the biblical statements on God's nature);
- Our *concept of God* becomes secular-romantic as well (since we project all of our secular images on God).

In the end, we wind up with an unreal God combined with a godless reality, a worldless faith and a faithless understanding of the world. It was the atheist philosopher Ludwig Feuerbach (and later, his follower Karl Marx) who accused Christianity of projecting its own, worldly images onto heaven and calling that self-created being "God." When the atheists declared that God is dead, they were absolutely right. *That* God is dead. In fact, that God has never existed.

Thank you Ludwig Feuerbach and Karl Marx for helping deliver us Christians from such an erroneous image of God!

### The God of the Bible

That is the reason why the whole first part of this book on loving relationships is dedicated to understanding the nature of God. Before we develop practical exercises for growing in love, we need to understand what we mean by love. Our standard for loving others is God's love for us.

If we study how God has put his love into action, we learn that love is more than just giving something to someone else. When God expresses his love toward us, he doesn't just give us *something,* he gives us *himself.* We will come back to the practical implications of this distinction in the section on "primary and secondary virtues" (pages 41-43).

> Our standard for loving others is God's love for us.

The essence of the Christian understanding of love is that we give *ourselves* away. This is, in no way, an easy concept. There is a price to be paid. However, at the same time, this is the key to experiencing a fulfilling, challenging, and happy life. Here, the paradox holds true, "Whoever finds his life will lose it; but whoever loses his life for my sake will find it" (Matt. 10:39).

I am aware that it may seem tedious to some readers to have to deal with concepts about God and his nature when reading a book on how to grow in love. I promise you that we will come to the nitty-gritty of real, down-to-earth details for growing in love (chapters 3 and 4 of this book deal exclusively with practical exercises). However, I hope that by the time we get there, you will appreciate the theological foundation on which the practical exercises have been built.

**Chapter 1:
Foundations**

# Three dimensions of God's love

*The Bible, in its original terminology, constantly summarizes the essence of God's character in terms of justice, truth, and grace.*

Take a look at the diagram on the right (page 21). The concept of love can be expressed in two different ways. We can use just *one* word, "love," in the center of the diagram (where we could also put the term "God"); or we can use *three* words, "justice," "truth," and "grace," that refer to different aspects of love. Of course, these three terms cannot be radically separated from each other; in reality, their meaning is overlapping. In fact, the more we reflect God's love, the more the meanings of these three terms merge.

If these terms are so central to understanding God's nature, we might ask why we can't come up with any Bible verses that summarize these three aspects in one sentence? Every Bible reader knows that Scripture speaks about each of these dimensions at length, but if it is true that the integration of justice, truth, and grace is a key spiritual issue, shouldn't we expect to find verses that make explicit reference to this *trio*?

## The problem of translation

The fact of the matter is that the Bible, in its original terminology, constantly summarizes the essence of God's character in terms of justice, truth, and grace. The reason why most of us

*The three terms* **'æmunah** *(truth),* **sedaqah** *(justice), and* **hæsæd** *(grace) are used together throughout the book of Psalms when it comes to praising God. In most of our Bible translations, however, the terms have been rendered differently (below, NIV).*

| Psalm 33:4-5 | For the word of the Lord is right and true; he is *faithful* (**'æmunah**) in all he does. The Lord loves *righteousness* (**sedaqah**) and justice; the earth is full of his unfailing *love* (**hæsæd**). |
|---|---|
| Psalm 36:5-6 | Your *love* (**hæsæd**), O Lord, reaches to the heavens, your *faithfulness* (**'æmunah**) to the skies. Your *righteousness* (**sedaqah**) is like the mighty mountains, your justice like the great deep. |
| Psalm 40:10 | I do not hide your *righteousness* (**sedaqah**) in my heart; I speak of your faithfulness and salvation. I do not conceal your *love* (**hæsæd**) and your *truth* (**'æmunah**) from the great assembly. |
| Psalm 88:11-12 | Is your *love* (**hæsæd**) declared in the grave, your *faithfulness* (**'æmunah**) in destruction? Are your wonders known in the place of darkness, or your *righteous* (**sedaqah**) deeds in the land of oblivion? |
| Psalm 98:2-3 | The Lord has made his salvation known and revealed his *righteousness* (**sedaqah**) to the nations. He has remembered his *love* (**hæsæd**) and his *faithfulness* (**'æmunah**) to the house of Israel. |
| Psalm 119:75-76 | I know, O Lord, that your laws are *righteous* (**sedaqah**), and in *faithfulness* (**'æmunah**) you have afflicted me. May your unfailing *love* (**hæsæd**) be my comfort. |

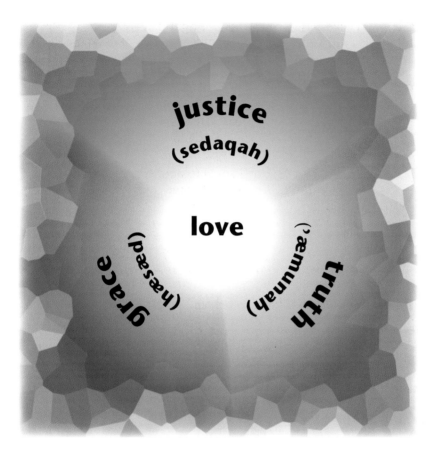

*We can express it in one word, love (in the very center), or we can express it by using three different terms (justice, truth, grace), each one covering a different aspect of God's love. When dealing with these terms, however, we should go back to their original Hebrew meaning, which may differ considerably from the everyday usage of the terms in our own language.*

aren't familiar with this terminology, is simply that the terms have been translated differently. For instance, look at the table on the left (page 20). I have selected six passages from the Psalms (that are representative of countless others), each of them containing an explicit reference to God's justice, truth, and grace. When you read most English translations of these texts, you will observe that though in most cases all three terms are used, they are seldom found in the same passage. Why?

### Oriental versus Western paradigms

The answer lies in the fact that in Hebrew (which is not only the language of the Old Testament, but also the conceptual background of Jesus and the apostles) these terms have a meaning that is hard to translate adequately into other languages. In some languages it is difficult to communicate the exact "flavor" of these terms, especially in those that have been strongly influenced by the Greek heritage (for instance, many of the Indo-European or "Western" languages). Just take a look at the individual terms:

- **'æmunah**, the Hebrew word for truth, is sometimes translated as "truth," sometimes as "faithfulness." As we will see later (pages 32-33), it is characteristic not only for Hebrew, but for many non-Western languages, to use one term that covers "both" aspects.

• **sedaqah**, the term for justice, is sometimes translated as "righteousness," which is another nuance of the rich meaning of the biblical term.

• **hæsæd**, the term for grace, is frequently translated "love." This seems to be a consequence of the exclusively "soft love concept" mentioned above. If love is reduced to certain aspects of grace, the next logical step is to use the word "love" in order to translate the Hebrew word for "grace."

> Countless Christians place special emphasis on one of the three aspects, since that one has special significance to them.

### Three relational terms

It is noteworthy that in Hebrew (as well as in other Middle Eastern languages), these three words are relational. Thus *justice* doesn't relate primarily to the "objective fairness" associated with a court of law. It includes a genuine compassion for others that goes beyond legal justice. *Truth*, when put into practice, implies trustworthiness and cannot be reduced to mere honesty. *Grace* is based on a relationship of acceptance. It is more than just forgiveness. According to the Bible, it literally includes giving yourself.

In Western languages these three terms can be easily separated one from another. In Middle Eastern languages this is more difficult. However, since Western (Greek/Indo-European) thought has shaped Christian theology more than Eastern thought throughout church history, Christianity today suffers from an isolated rather than an integrated view. Countless Christians stress primarily one of the three aspects, since that one has special significance to them. But we can only practice the three values *in love* if we integrate all of them. If we fail to do this, though we might still practice justice, truth, or grace, we have failed to truly love.

*The diagram below highlights the relational nature of the terms justice, truth, and grace.*

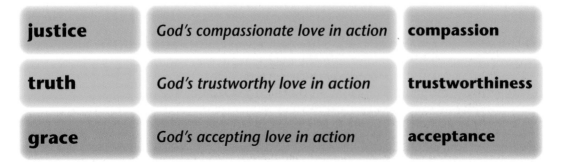

| justice | God's compassionate love in action | compassion |
| truth | God's trustworthy love in action | trustworthiness |
| grace | God's accepting love in action | acceptance |

# God is light

I n our cross-cultural ministry, it is a constant challenge to find images that aren't too culturally bound, and communicate universally. There are far fewer images of this kind than one might assume. However, there is at least *one* image that has been used throughout the centuries in various cultures and religions, including Christianity—the image of light. It is a truly universal metaphor for life, wholeness, and happiness, whereas darkness symbolizes sin, deceit, and death.

While in many religions this metaphor has been used in highly speculative ways, it is characteristic of biblical teaching that it is devoid of any esoteric connotations. John, especially, used the imagery of light and darkness throughout his writings, culminating in the sentence, "God is light, and in him there is no darkness at all" (1 John 1:5). In the same way, Jesus calls himself "the light of the world" (John 8:12). Thus we can be challenged to "believe in the light" and to become "sons of the light" ourselves (John 12:36), which means no more nor less than reflecting the divine light in our own lives.

### An inter-cultural metaphor

In the trinitarian paradigm of Natural Church Development, I have given this metaphor a central place, since it can help us understand complex theological realities in an easy-to-grasp way. Just as light that falls through a prism fans out into the different colors of the spectrum, the light of God can be perceived by us humans in various ways. Some people might see green, others red, others blue—yet we all encounter the same God (see graphic below).

**Just as light that falls through a prism fans out into the different colors of the spectrum, the light of God can be perceived in various ways.**

the light of justice

the light of grace

God = love = light

the light of truth

the light of love

*The metaphor of light is frequently used throughout the Bible. While 1 John 4:8 states that "God is love," we read in 1 John 1:5, "God is light." Considering the terms "light" and "love" in relationship to each other opens up helpful vantage points from which to understand the dynamics of how God's love is spread. In essence, we reflect God's light rather than producing our own lights.*

*The light metaphor is often used to describe the different aspects of God's love. In Isaiah 51:4 we read, "My **justice** will become a light to the nations." Psalm 43:3 presents a prayer for God's "light and **truth**." Psalm 112:4 states that even in darkness light dawns for the "**gracious** man." It's always the same light shining, even if we perceive different shades of it at different times.*

The graphic also reveals that, the closer we are to the center, the better we are able to reflect God's love. The further we move away from the center, the darker the colors get. There are still traces of God's light even in those remote places, but the further we get from the center, the more the light of God's love gets diffracted and dimmed.

### The colors of light

What is light? In the world that God has created, light is nothing other than color. It is important to notice that the colors of light (self-luminous colors) function differently than object colors. When we mix object colors (such as oil or water colors), the presence of all colors results in black, while the absence of all colors is white—an empty canvas. Self-luminous colors function the other way around: white is the result of the presence of all colors, while black is the absence of any color. In the color white, the whole spectrum of light is reflected. The brighter the light, the more powerful the reflection.

> The colors of light function differently than object colors. White is the result of the presence of all colors; black, the absence of any color.

Those of us who work on computers are accustomed to these dynamics, since that is how images are projected on a computer screen. In order to display a picture in full color, the screen has to project red, green, and blue. If one color is missing, the image is distorted (see pictures to the right).

### Light in Hebrew and Greek thought

It is interesting to note that in biblical times, the Greek and Hebrew cultures had a somewhat different view of color and light, a difference that can still be observed when comparing Western and Oriental cultures today. For the Greeks, color played a more important role; for the Israelites, it was light. When it came to color, the Hebrews especially appreciated white and red, since they were closest to fire light.

While in Western cultures (that are based on the Greek heritage) a concrete form is indispensable in the representation of beauty, in the Hebrew paradigm one of the highest kinds of beauty was seen in the formless fire—the life-giving light. This observation has helped me understand how different cultures function. Whatever our cultural heritage might be, light *and* color, energy *and* form, the dynamic *and* the static are parts of the reality God has created. Thus we try to integrate both poles in our three-color paradigm.

### What does the light metaphor imply?

As religious history has proven, the imagery of light is so powerful that it can be easily used—and misused—for wild speculations on the nature of God. Therefore it is important to carefully consider what the biblical statements communicate about light. In the context of this book, the following biblical truths about light are the most relevant:

Green missing

Red missing

Blue missing

Green, red, and blue complete

*To display a photo-graph on a com-puter screen, the three colors red, green, and blue are needed. If one color is miss-ing, the picture is incomplete— a distorted view of reality (first three photographs). Only when all three colors are displayed is the pic-ture complete (last photograph).*

- It is certainly no coincidence that the first thing God created was light (Gen. 1:3). Light is the precondition of life. It illuminates, reveals truth, destroys illusions, shows us the path we must take. At the same time, it heals, warms, and nurtures.

- Probably the most practical consequence of understanding God and his love in terms of "light" is to show us clearly our human job description. We are to reflect the divine light. The Bible speaks about "walking in the light" (1 John 1:7). In John's writings, "know-ing God" is a synonym of "living in the light," which again is a synonym for "living in God's love." The proof that we actually live in the light—metaphorically speaking—is that all three colors of God's love are visible in our lives.

- The light metaphor is also helpful when it comes to understanding its "opposite." Darkness is nothing other than the absence of light. It doesn't have any power of its own. The practical conclusions are obvious. How can we fight against the manifestations of darkness, such as sin and heresy? By spreading the light! Where light shines, darkness has no place. It disappears "all by itself." In the three-color paradigm of Natural Church Development, we consistently try to apply these dynamics to the daily lives of churches—with highly encouraging results.

# What is darkness?

Darkness is the absence of light—no more, no less. Thus it is not really appropriate to present darkness as the "opposite" of light. That would suggest that it has the same power as light. But darkness cannot shine like light can; rather, it disappears the moment the first glimmer of light emerges. Therefore, the most precise definition of darkness would probably be "non-light." As such, however, it is still an important part of reality.

It is not true that people who live in darkness have no knowledge at all. They can see reality, but without divine light they are in danger of having a distorted view. Things will be out of proportion or out of balance. Small things appear big and big ones, small; meaningless goals appear divine and divine goals, meaningless. The less access people have to the light of God's love, the more they create artificial lights that merely decorate the darkness. These artificial lights just add to the sense of confusion.

> The less people have access to the light of God's love, the more they create artificial lights that decorate the darkness.

### Darkness inside and outside the church

The New Testament frequently uses the term "darkness" to describe reality outside the Christian faith. However, it also speaks of darkness inside the church and in the life of the individual believer. The Christian faith is a constant battle to bring light, which both reveals and heals, to areas of darkness.

In my opinion, the darkness within the church has always been a greater problem than the darkness in the world. Lies disguise themselves as piety. Clear manifestations of sin are presented as expressions of God's love. Jesus rightly warned, "If your eyes are bad, your whole body will be full of darkness. If then the light within you is darkness, how great is that darkness!" (Matt. 6:23).

### Three manifestations of darkness

Take a look at the diagram on the right (page 27). As we have seen before, people who want to live in the light should not separate the three dimensions of justice, truth, and grace. However, it is easy to focus on one or two of these components, and forget about the others. This kind of imbalance can take place in all three directions, with equally dramatic consequences. Look at the three expressions of darkness outside the black circle:

- The first is *deception.* This is the result of stressing justice and grace, but bypassing truth. We could have also chosen the word "lie," however, since people are more often victims of lies rather than being personally responsible for them, the broader term "deception" better identifies this particular danger.

- The second expression of darkness is *mercilessness.* This is frequently seen in groups that stress both justice and truth, but lack a practical

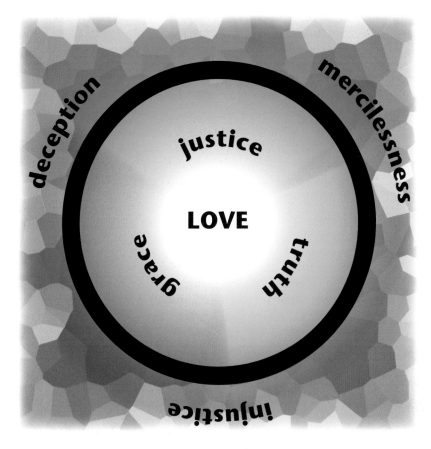

*This diagram shows that heresy is not necessarily the opposite of biblical standards, but is often something far more difficult to detect: a partial truth. One aspect of the biblical message is presented as an absolute, while neglecting other aspects. The three terms outside of the black circle (deception, mercilessness, and injustice) reveal what happens when we fail to integrate one of the three components of love.*

understanding of grace. They might have the "right" topics on their agenda, but rather than communicating them in a spirit of grace, their fight for biblical goals comes across as hard-hearted, harsh, and intolerant.

- The third danger is *injustice*. This is found in groups that emphasize truth and grace, but fail to consider justice. It's amazing how often people, in the name of truth and grace, resist movements that strive for social justice (usually by demanding grace toward those people in power and thus benefiting from unjust conditions).

When we look at these groups, there is no doubt that all of them have biblical values on their agenda. But since they fail to integrate the three dimensions of justice, truth, and grace, their activities become unloving. Yes, you can be a social activist, an advocate of the truest truth, or the most gracious person on planet earth—and still miss the center of biblical faith: love. Striving for biblical balance will make every believer more mature, more effective, and more Christ-like.

<table>
<tr><td>Chapter 1:<br>Foundations</td></tr>
</table>

# Practicing love means reflecting God's light

Jesus not only called himself "the light of the world" (John 8:12); he also used the same terminology in his Sermon on the Mount to describe his disciples: *they* are "the light of the world" (Matt. 5:14). Does this imply that there are two lights of the world? Yes and no. Metaphorically speaking, Jesus is the sun, his disciples are the moon. Both shed light, so the effect is similar. However, the sun is the source of the light, and the moon merely reflects the light that it receives from the sun. When we see the "moonlight" at night, we should never forget that we are still seeing the "light of the sun."

> Once you know where your color deficiencies are, you will be able to clean your mirror and reflect God's love more fully.

### Before giving, we must receive

The Bible communicates the very same truth in a plethora of different ways: You can only give away what you have previously received; in order to share God's love with others, you first have to be filled with his love. Love should not be confused with the doing of "good deeds" in one's own strength. Rather, it requires living in the love you have received and allowing it to permeate your whole being. 1 John 4:19 is probably the shortest description of this principle: "We love because he first loved us."

### The New Commandment

Jesus continually communicated these dynamics to his disciples. The climax of his teaching on love is recorded in John 13:34-35: "A new command I give you: Love one another.

---

### Contemporary examples for justice, truth, and grace

Over the next few pages, I will illustrate each of the three dimensions of love with examples of Christians who lived in the past century and became famous for their achievements in a specific area (be it justice, truth, or grace). I have always been **reluctant to present "big names"** as models, since I have too often experienced the counterproductive effects of this approach:

- The models are usually presented in a "blissful" light, ignoring the less favorable aspects of their character. As a result we put them (at least psychologically) almost on the same level as Jesus, not remembering that they were **imperfect and lopsided** in many respects, just as all of us are imperfect and lopsided human beings.

- Consequently, we tend to **revere these heroes** ("Isn't it great that we had people like them: so courageous, so smart, so gracious?"), rather than identifying with their agenda and applying the values they stood for to our own lives.

Having said this, however, I believe that real-life examples can help us to understand that the biblical values that are shared in this book are highly relevant for our times and, more importantly, literally have the **potential to change the world**.

As I have loved you, so you must love one another. By this all men will know that you are my disciples, if you love one another." In a way, these two verses are a summary of Jesus' whole mission. Let's have a brief look at the three key ingredients of this passage:

- First, Jesus *introduces* his message as a "new command." In his day, there were 613 commandments in Jewish law, 365 negative ones and 248 positive ones. "New" definitely didn't mean that Jesus was now adding commandment number 614. The new thing about this command was that it encompassed all of the others and revealed their deepest meaning (compare Matt. 22:40). That was revolutionary, indeed. Rather than concerning yourself with hundreds of details, focus on one essential thing!

**You can only give away what you have received before.**

- Second, he presents the *content* of his message: "As I have loved you, so you must love one another." It's characteristic of Jesus' teaching to give not only the command to love, but also to relate that command to his own love for his disciples. In other words: "Gentlemen, never forget this: Here is the source, and there is the river. Here is the sun, and there is the moon."

- Third, he predicted the *effect* of his message: "By this all men will know that you are my disciples." By their *love* the disciples would be recognized as God's people. What is the result? Many will be drawn to become disciples themselves. To put it into our cold, abstract, statistical NCD slang: "If the love quotient of a church is high, the church will grow numerically." Isn't it amazing that one of the pivotal conclusions of the most comprehensive research of this kind ever done simply confirms what Jesus taught 2000 years ago?

### What are your problem areas?

The goal of this book is to help us put Jesus' teaching into practice. It is focused on the New Commandment which is, indeed, nothing less than a summary of the biblical message in its entirety. The aim is not to produce loving actions in our own strength, but to reflect the light of God's love. The Christian mystics liked to use the image of a mirror to communicate this truth: A mirror can only reflect when it has first been cleaned. This is the deepest background of the many "purification" practices that we can find in these groups: to become a more effective mirror for reflecting God's light.

In the next few pages, we'll take a closer look at each of the three dimensions of love, and then ask ourselves the following question: In which of these areas is my own mirror smudged, so that I'm not reflecting a specific color of God's light as adequately and fully as I could? Once you know where your color deficiencies are, you will be able to clean your mirror and reflect God's love more fully than before.

# The color green: justice

Contrary to a widespread misunderstanding of the term, justice— as portrayed in the Bible—can take sides. It has little to do with the unaffected neutrality that many of us associate with the term and even project on God: a funny mixture between a British judge and a German bureaucrat who constantly quotes jurisprudence in order to make life much more complicated than it ought to be. Justice in the Bible is something altogether different. It is the active expression of God's compassionate love. It takes sides for those who need it most: the underprivileged and the suffering, the weak and the poor. Justice is far more than applying laws. It aims at a morality over and above the legal code.

> Justice puts God's compassionate love into action. It takes sides with the underprivileged and suffering.

### The core value: compassion

The Latin term *compassio* has always represented a central value in the social justice tradition of Christianity. *Compassio* in its original sense means suffering together with the cruci- fied Christ. It is Christ himself who is seen in the countless victims of injustice (see Matt. 25:31-46). Thus, serving these people and helping them receive fair treatment, is seen as a direct ministry to Christ. Jesus' Sermon on the Mount out- lines a very precise program of the kind of justice that God has in mind.

Jesus taught us to consider "poor Lazarus" as our primary example in the quest for justice (Luke 16:19-31). It is this perspective that many of those who have never suffered from injustice are entirely unaware of.

---

### Contemporary example: Martin Luther King (1929-1968)

This Baptist pastor became a worldwide symbol for **nonviolent resistance** against unjust laws which, in his day, affected the African-American population of the United States. His core principle was to counter violence with non-violence, hatred with love. "Darkness cannot drive out darkness," he preached, "only light can do that. **Hate cannot drive out hate**; only love can do that." His strategy of civil disobedience implied con- sciously disobeying unjust laws while peacefully accepting the penalty for it. This took him to prison innumerable times. "There are two types of laws: just and unjust," he said. "One has not only a legal but a moral responsibility to obey just laws. Conversely, one has a moral **responsibility to disobey** unjust laws." When his opponents accused him of being an extremist, he replied, "Was not Jesus an extremist for love? Was not Amos an **extremist for justice**? So the question is not whether we will be extremists, but what kind of extremists we will be. Will we be extremists for hate or for love? Will we be extremists for the preservation of injustice or for the extension of justice?"

To this day, King remains a **controversial figure**. Many see him as a model for Chris- tian action in politics and one of the martyrs of our times; others criticize him for his "insurgent views" and a life-style "inconsistent with biblical standards."

*Justice (represented by the color green) is one of three indispensable dimensions of God's love. However, it must be supplemented by truth (red) and grace (blue) in order to maintain balance.*

## Focus on society

People who are committed to justice—in biblical times as well as today—are usually controversial people. They upset those who benefit from the status quo. They live in tension with representatives of the state, the military, and the business world. For example, the founder of the Quakers (one of the churches at the very center of the social justice tradition), made the principle of *egalité* a feature of his personal life long before the French Revolution. He consistently treated everyone—rich and poor, powerful and weak—alike: no titles, no bowing down, no symbols of reverence. Initially, American soldiers who became Quakers were not rejected because of their pacifism, but because of their alleged "disrespect" for their officers.

The Old Testament clearly demonstrates that justice has an affinity to the social and political dimension of the faith (as seen in many of the prophetic books, especially Amos). Justice not only sees individuals in their misery, but it also inquires after the causes of that misery. It is focused on society and its structures.

**Chapter 1: Foundations**

# The color red: truth

One of the early meanings of the Greek term for truth, *aletheia*, was to tear away a veil. Truth is "unveiled reality"; reality as seen through God's eyes. The Apostle John liked to combine this concept of truth with one of his favorite terms, light: "Whoever lives by the truth comes into the light" (John 3:21). Where the light of truth shines, revelation happens, deception disappears, and reality becomes visible.

The light of truth exposes lies where they would otherwise go unnoticed, which may be painful. It is tempting to avoid confrontation and justify that decision in the name of "love": "I don't want to hurt the other person's feelings." However, our hesitation to confront often has little to do with our concern for the other person. Rather, we are concerned about our *own* feelings. We don't like to confront others because we fear rejection and don't relish the difficult task of walking beside them through the process of change. Thus it is understandable that we try to avoid communicating the truth. But this should never be done in the name of love. One of the indispensable components of love is to minister truth to other people.

> Truth puts God's trustworthy love into action. It reveals reality as seen through God's eyes.

### The core value: trustworthiness

There is a second aspect to the biblical concept of truth that comes out of the Hebrew term for truth, which can also be translated "faithfulness." While according to Greek thought you can *show* the truth, *speak* the truth, and *teach* the truth, it is characteristic of the Hebrew mindset to *do* the truth. The use of this terminology in John 3:21 is a good example of this.

### Contemporary example: Francis Schaeffer (1912-1984)

Francis Schaeffer was one of the most influential advocates of "right belief"—the "**true truth**," as he liked to put it—that the last century has seen. "We not only believe in the existence of truth, but we believe **we have the truth**," he wrote. And he continued, "Do you think our contemporaries will take us seriously if we do not practice truth?" This conviction made him a **man of conversation**. His community L'Abri in the Swiss Alps was his response to the hippie communes that desperately sought community and meaning. Schaeffer's extensive understanding of the Bible was combined with a **critical study of the world of man,** including philosophy, history, culture, and the arts. He analyzed the roots of modern thinking in its rejection of rationality and strongly argued for **rationalism** in apologetics. Probably his greatest gift was his ability to communicate extremely complicated philosophical and theological issues on a non-technical level. Schaeffer's commitment to the unity of truth reinforced his lifetime insistence that the **Bible was inerrant** in all respects.

While many admired him for his exceptional encyclopedic knowledge and his facility in communicating the truth, especially to young people, others criticized him for imposing **a far too rationalistic grid** on Christianity.

*Truth (represented by the color red) is one of three indispensable dimensions of God's love. However, it must be supplemented by grace (blue) and justice (green) in order to maintain balance.*

The Hebrews weren't so concerned with what is true in the objective sense, but with what is reliable in an existential sense. In Exodus 1:19, for instance, we learn that the midwives clearly told a lie (according to Western thought!) in order to protect human life. In Hebrew thought, as in many other Oriental cultures, this wouldn't even be called a lie. According to them, a lie is that which is powerless, empty, and vain. A spring that gives no water "lies" (Isa. 58:11). In essence, this concept of truth calls us to be reliable, to be trustworthy, to do what we are meant to do.

### Focus on both the Bible and reality

Truth, in the Christian sense, has a dual focus. One is the word of God, the other is reality. Christians who are strong in truth do not usually feel threatened when others challenge their views. On the other hand, people who are weakly rooted in truth regularly find themselves on the defensive and often develop an unspiritual fanaticism. When one is strong in the biblical understanding of truth, the opposite is true: you enjoy questioning yourself, *your* views, *your* traditions, *your* values, in order to give more and more room to the light of truth in your life.

# The color blue: grace

While truth may require removing veils from reality, unmasking people to reveal who they really are, grace may well imply respecting those veils if they shelter the shame, mystery, or dignity of a person. To understand what grace is all about, it's worthwhile to meditate on the New Testament term *charis*. It's the root from which the English word "charming" stems. Actually, *charis* has a lot to do with charm: It can refer either to physical beauty or to a winsome attitude that radiates warmth, acceptance, and joy.

> Grace puts God's accepting love into action. It's a winsome attitude that radiates warmth, acceptance, and joy.

The biblical concept of grace contradicts a widespread understanding of justice. And, in fact, grace isn't always just. Why does a father throw a party for his son who has squandered his wealth in wild living rather than for the older son who has served his father faithfully all along? Grace is an undeserved, free gift. Christians who live and die for high moral standards often reject a radical application of the principle of grace. They have paid a great price to become members of what they hoped was an exclusive club, the church. Now they want to keep it as exclusive as possible. They regard grace as unfair.

### The core value: acceptance

While Jesus may never have used the term, he constantly modeled grace. From him we learn the true extent of forgiveness: not seven times, but 77 times (Matt. 18:22). A wonderful case study of grace in action is Jesus' encounter with the Samaritan woman at the well (John 4). We learn that while grace in no way justifies sin, it does accept the sinner. And

### Contemporary example: Mother Teresa (1910-1997)

The ministry of this Roman-Catholic nun was focused on the **poorest of the poor**: the incurably ill and the outcast, the dying and the victims of AIDS. This focus also made her an advocate for the unborn. While acknowledging the impact of unjust political structures, her own ministry exclusively targeted **helping the individual**. One of her core values was not only to minister unselfishly, but **"to do it with a smile."** The motto that she taught her co-workers was, "Never allow yourself to meet someone who will not be happier after their encounter with you." An American journalist recalled sitting behind Mother Teresa watching how she tenderly washed a dying, worm-ridden person. "I wouldn't do that for a million dollars," the journalist said. Mother Teresa responded with this short, profound answer: "Neither would I." Later on, she added, "I see in every human being the helpless Jesus. Therefore, **I can do it for free**." When invited by wealthy organizations, her message was, "We don't need your money, we need your time. We want you **to give yourself** to the poor."

While for many people Mother Teresa has become a worldwide symbol of Christian mercy, others have criticized her for **not addressing the social structures** that produced the poverty she sought to address.

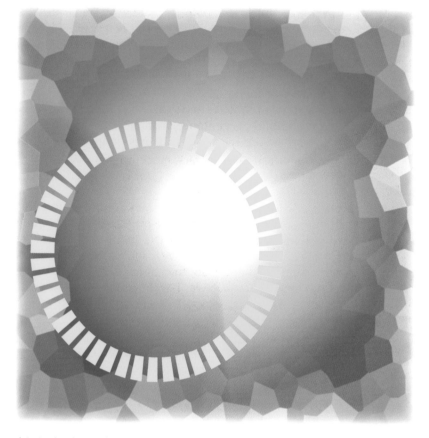

*Grace (represented by the color blue) is one of three indispensable dimensions of God's love. However, it must be supplemented by justice (green) and truth (red) in order to maintain balance.*

this is the key: The sense of being accepted enables people to open up their hearts, and show us who they really are. Acceptance is far more than mere tolerance. It embraces a person regardless of his or her condition, and then helps that person mature.

## Focus on the individual

Grace focuses on the individual. It looks at people through the eyes of Jesus. As a result, it not only sees their present situation, but also their God-given potential and future possibilities. When you encounter Christian leaders who aren't rooted in grace, you may admire them for their achievements, but you usually feel very small in their presence. On the other hand, with leaders who radiate grace, the opposite happens: Though initially one might approach them feeling small, helpless, and unimportant, afterwards you sense that *you* have grown considerably.

We must never forget that as Christians we have not only been saved by grace, we must also live by grace. Our failure to do this seems to be the number one reason for the emotional and relational problems that can be detected in so many churches.

# Three models of love in action

O ver the next few pages, I want to expand on the three dimensions of God's love with reference to the teachings of three biblical authors: James as a model for justice, John as a model for truth, and Paul as a model for grace. Although each one has become especially well-known for his emphasis on one of the three dimensions, all of them are good illustrations of how to balance justice, truth, and grace.

### Different messages for different people

Thousands of pages have been written by the most brilliant scholars about "contradictions" in the messages of James, John, and Paul. In fact, Martin Luther was so convinced of the theological contradiction between James and Paul that he promised to give his doctor's cap to the person who could make their messages sing the same tune.

Let's face it. James, John, and Paul definitely did *not* say the same thing. Each of them was addressing a unique situation that was in need of a unique message. James stressed *justice* because he was addressing second-generation Christians whose moral vigor had faded. John stressed *truth* because he was warning Christians against certain heresies. Paul stressed *grace* because he was dealing with teachers who were trying to re-introduce the judaistic system of righteousness.

> It is helpful to think of James, John and Paul as church consultants who were addressing the color deficiencies of their respective audiences.

Take a look at the picture on the left. Are the different figures walking in the same, or in different (even opposite) directions? Do they need the same, or different (opposite) instructions for reaching their destination? Think about it for a moment. If you have found the answer, you have also found the answer to the theological debate mentioned above.

### Ministering to different minimum factors

One of the most basic principles our NCD consultants are taught is that they should focus on the "minimum factor" of each church they work with, rather than promoting their own favorite suggestions. If they were to take the same recommendations to every church, they would do a disastrous job as consultants. It is helpful to think of James, John and Paul as church consultants who were addressing the color deficiencies of their respective audiences—because this is what they were doing!

If you had the opportunity to see me teach in different settings, you could easily detect the same sort of "contradictions" that scholars have identified when studying James, John and Paul. Is this because I am opportunistic, communicating what a specific group wants to hear? No. The opposite is true. I don't focus on the topics that are most *popular* in a given group, but on those that they most need to hear—their "color deficiencies." Guess from whom I have learned this?

Ladies and gentlemen, please give a warm welcome to James, John, and Paul! We sorely need their messages.

# Model for justice: James

James, an earthly brother of Jesus and one of the pillars of the first church in Jerusalem, passionately kept the Jewish law even after he became a Christian. The early church historian, Eusebius, records that James "used to enter the temple alone and be found kneeling and praying for forgiveness for the people, until his knees grew hard like a camel's because of his constant worship of God. Due to his excessive righteousness he was called 'the Just.'"

## James' message: "Do what the word says"

The letter that carries his name contains nothing that cannot be found elsewhere in the Bible. In form, it follows the tradition of Old Testament wisdom literature. In content, it is very similar to the gospel of Matthew, particularly to Jesus' Sermon on the Mount (Matt. 5-7). The core message of his teaching is, "Do not merely listen to the word, and so deceive yourselves. Do what it says" (James 1:22). In contrast to other books of the Bible, however, James puts this message at the very center of his letter. He loves the imperative verb form (do it!); in the 108 verses of his letter we find 54 imperatives.

James does not attack an intellectual heresy, but a practical heresy that can well occur in conjunction with orthodox doctrine. He is interested in a faith that shows itself in practical acts of love, and therefore stresses that "faith without action is dead" (James 2:17). His goal is to drive out the worldly spirit that has infected the church (James 4:4). He is especially concerned that the poor and needy have been treated unfairly (James 5:4-6) and that the wealthy have been granted special privileges (James 2:1-7). According to James, this kind of partiality is unacceptable in the church of Jesus Christ.

*Since James was addressing second-generation Christians whose moral vigor had faded, he stressed the importance of justice (green segment) in pursuit of a holistic understanding of love.*

## Who needs James?

All of us are in need of repeated exposure to James' message; however, his teaching is especially beneficial for:

- upper-middle-class churches that have become so comfortable in their cushy armchairs that they have forgotten about the needs of the "Lazarus" on the street.

- churches where the rich and famous receive special treatment.

- churches that have allowed their "openmindedness" to reduce biblical standards so that the church fits the spirit of the times.

- churches that are characterized by an intellectual orthodoxy that merely influences the minds, but not the daily lives of the believers.

- churches whose slant on grace has actually begun to justify sin rather than help the sinner get rid of unbiblical behavior.

Chapter 1:
Foundations

# Model for truth: John

There is a widespread image of the Apostle John that portrays him as a gentle, tolerant, and amiable person. From all we know about the historical John, he was just the opposite. There were good reasons why Jesus called him a "Son of Thunder," a nickname that fits well with the impulsive, stormy, demanding description of him in the gospels. It is noteworthy that it is John, more than the other gospel writers, who highlights the severe side of Jesus: calling the Jews children of the devil (John 8:41-45), accusing the Pharisees of spiritual blindness (John 9:39-41), describing his predecessors as thieves and robbers (John 10:8). Tough words!

### John's message: "Walk in the truth"

When we look at John's recommendations for dealing with people who teach falsehood, we certainly wouldn't regard them as especially tolerant, either: "If anyone comes to you and does not bring this teaching, do not take him into your house or welcome him. Anyone who welcomes him shares in his wicked work" (2 John 10-11). It is told that John consistently practiced what he preached. When he heard that the heretic Cerinth was in the same public bath house as himself, he immediately ran out of the bath. The historian Eusebius reports that he couldn't stand to be under the same roof as "the enemy of the truth."

On the basis of this account, how could the "soft" image of John emerge? The answer is simple. John's gospel and his letters speak more about love than other books of the Bible. If our own concept of love is exclusively soft, we will project this softness onto John's writings and thus create our own "soft Johnny." But John's focus, when writing about love, was primarily on the dimension of truth. "I have no greater joy," he wrote, "than to hear that my children are walking in the truth" (3 John 4). "If we claim to have fellowship with God yet walk in the darkness, we lie and do not live by the truth" (1 John 1:6).

*John had to cope with heretics that were increasingly becoming a danger to the church. For that reason, his writings focused on how Christian love can express itself in truth (red segment).*

When reading his writings, it is evident that John's focus on the truth, even his harshness toward any form of heresy, was motivated by love. He knew well what the effects of heresy are, that it can literally destroy people's lives. That explains his passion for the truth.

### Who needs John?

All of us need to be repeatedly exposed to John's message; however, his teaching is especially beneficial for:

• churches that have adopted a relativistic view of truth.

• churches that have more of a secular understanding of love than a biblical one.

• churches that have put "truth" at the top of their agenda, but don't seem to see its inner connection to love.

• churches that have been affected by false teachings without even noticing it.

# Model for grace: Paul

P aul has rightly received the title, "Apostle of Grace." While he does write about justice and truth as well, we get the sense that, when it comes to grace, we meet the "real Paul." The term is mentioned 156 times in the New Testament; and 100 of these instances are found in Paul's writings alone. Every one of his letters starts by striking the note of grace (at least by the second sentence), and ends by leaving the sound of grace ringing in our ears. And the message in between?

## Paul's message: "All is grace and grace is for all"

Paul knew who he had been (a persecutor of the church) and what he had become (an apostle of Jesus Christ), and he could only give one explanation for it: grace. "I am the least of the apostles and do not even deserve to be called an apostle, because I persecuted the church of God. But by the grace of God I am what I am, and his grace to me was not without effect" (1 Cor. 15:9-10). Paul knew better than anyone that grace is exclusively traced back to God's initiative. There is nothing we can do to make God love us more. Grace is an expression of God's *unconditional* love.

His passion for grace explains his equal passion to fight teachings that would undermine grace. He calls them "a different gospel, which is really no gospel at all" (Gal. 1:6-7). To the Galatians, who had started to follow these doctrines, he writes, "You foolish Galatians! Who has bewitched you?" (Gal. 3:1). Paul knew what was at stake if grace were removed from the center of one's understanding of God's love.

It's important to note that, according to Paul, we are not only saved by grace, but we are also called by grace. It is certainly no accident that the key term used by Paul for gift-oriented ministry—*charisma*—has the same root as the term for grace, *charis*. In Greek, the suffix *-ma* at the end of a word usually describes the effect of the word in front of the *-ma*. So what are spiritual gifts? They are the effect of grace in our lives. They are God's grace in action.

*Paul's controversy with legalistic groups forms the background of many of his letters. His remedy? A radical focus on grace (blue segment).*

## Who needs Paul?

All of us need repeated exposure to Paul's message; however, his teaching is especially beneficial for:

- churches in which the appeal to grace is part of their doctrine, but its practical meaning for the believers has been lost.
- churches that have become proud of themselves and their achievements.
- churches that are truly committed to the Great Commission but have lost the balance between receiving and giving and have burned out their members.
- churches that have legalistic tendencies (note that there are evangelical, charismatic, and liberal varieties of legalism).

**Chapter 1: Foundations**

# What does this mean in practice?

A mature, loving person is able to express love in a wide variety of ways, depending on the need of the moment. If you have only learned to express love in *one* specific way, you will only be able to respond appropriately to a very limited number of situations. Outside of these settings your typical love pattern may be useless or, even worse, counterproductive.

Sometimes love must be tough; other times, it can be tender. Sometimes we need to put on our rose-colored glasses, deliberately overlooking the less favorable aspects of someone's character. At other times, however, we need to focus on the negative in order to help people grow. If we always respond in the same way, because that is comfortable for *us*, we may end up expressing thoughtlessness, but definitely not love.

*Training your "love muscles" includes leaving your comfort zone.*

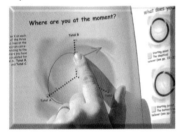

### Two criteria for ministering love

What is the most important color—or expression of love—in a given situation? To answer this question, we need to consider two primary issues:

1. What does the other person most need in this situation? Would it be an expression of justice, of truth, or of grace?

2. What am I able to offer at this time? For example, you might sense that the other person primarily needs to experience God's grace, but that in your present circumstances, you are not able to minister grace effectively to them. This could be a hint that you need further training in this area.

### Leaving your comfort zone

Training your "love muscles" includes leaving your comfort zone every now and then. If you aren't willing to do that, you cannot mature in love. There will be topics in this book that you might view with a certain amount of skepticism since they are outside of your comfort zone. Look at the pictures and examples that I have—deliberately—chosen to characterize the three dimensions of love (pages 30-35):

- People involved in demonstrations and acts of civil disobedience: "Dear Lord, a nest of terrorists!"
- People focused on the absolutely binding authority of Scripture: "For heaven's sake, hard-core fundamentalists!"
- People focused on radiating the positive, energizing atmosphere of grace: "Spare us the warm fuzzies!"

Leaving our comfort zone is usually an unpleasant exercise in the short run. But the very thing that we experience as unpleasant in the short run lays the foundation for overwhelming fulfillment in the long run. And even if we don't need to display certain aspects of love in a given situation—wouldn't it be nice to know that we *could*, at any given moment?

# Primary and secondary virtues

In Natural Church Development, the distinction between "primary" and "secondary virtues" plays an important role. My criticism of some sectors of the church growth movement has been that they have focused too strongly on secondary issues such as management techniques, marketing methods, analysis of contextual factors, numerical goal setting, etc. Secondary virtues aren't bad things, but they should never be confused with primary virtues such as passionate spirituality, empowering leadership, or loving relationships. Once the primary virtues are highly developed in a given church, we might tackle some of the secondary virtues as well, but they still will only be—theologically, spiritually and strategically—of secondary importance.

One of the dangers of secondary virtues is that they can be performed without taking the primary virtues into consideration. This is the tragedy of many management seminars that focus on performance, time management, sales methods, profit, share holder value, etc. These topics are certainly not irrelevant, but they are classic examples of secondary virtues. As soon as they become the central focus, we are almost inevitably forced to build an enterprise that is extremely susceptible to collapse. Secondary virtues only work in the long run if they are deeply rooted in primary virtues.

**A focus on primary virtues will help you perceive others with new eyes. It will enable you to see things you have never seen before.**

### Appearance rather than being

A focus on secondary virtues tempts people to give more importance to how they *appear* in the eyes of others than to what they really *are*. Again, image is not an unimportant issue, especially if you project a negative exterior image that is at variance with your positive inner being. It's never wrong to add secondary virtues on top of highly developed primary virtues. But when secondary virtues take the place of primary virtues, we run into problems. Believe it or not, there are even seminars that are designed to teach unloving people how to give the impression that they are loving. Thankfully these techniques never really work.

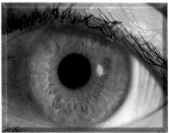

### Primary virtues and the three colors of love

Look at the diagram on page 43. You will see that each of the three colors has been assigned a pair of virtues, an "inner" virtue and an "outer" virtue. Both are important but they do not have the same value. In each case, the inner term represents the primary virtue; the outer one, a secondary virtue. While the primary virtues (compassion, trustworthiness, and acceptance) can only be practiced if you are rooted in love, the corresponding secondary virtues (fairness, honesty, and politeness) can be performed without love. It is characteristic of primary virtues that they are highly inter-related, i.e. you cannot really be "compassionate" in the best sense without being "trustworthy" and "accepting" as well. The secondary virtues, however, don't demonstrate this inter-relatedness.

### Why we focus on primary virtues

As is true of all Natural Church Development tools, this book deals exclusively with primary virtues. I am aware that there might be readers who will be disappointed by this approach. I have done "success seminars" where I have encountered people who have expected me to train them in what I would call "secondary virtues." The focus on primary virtues is, for them, far too slow, complicated, and unworkable in the "real world." How wrong they are: The major problem of the "real world" is, without a doubt, its one-sided focus on secondary virtues. In other words, the problems that the economic world of today suffers, are the very problems that it has produced itself—very carefully, very strategically, prepared in countless business meetings, documented in hundreds of books.

A focus on primary virtues will help you perceive others with new eyes. It will enable you to see things you have never seen before. A natural by-product will be greater success in all areas of your life, because you'll be grounded in principles, not in performance. Today's world desperately needs more people like that!

### Secondary virtues and money

Many people did not understand why Mother Teresa, when invited by wealthy organizations, liked to provoke her audiences with the message, "We don't need your money, we need your time. We want you to give yourself to the poor" (see page 34). Once we become aware of the dangers of focusing on secondary virtues, we might better understand the wisdom behind her words. Mother Teresa stubbornly resisted becoming part of the "secondary virtues game": by simply donating some money you are rewarded with the message that you have made some great contribution toward a better world. Even if we are surrounded today by a plethora of options for living the Christian life almost completely on a "secondary virtue" level, what Jesus wants from us is our heart, our love, our life.

**Research shows that too many traffic signs can be the cause of accidents.**

### Too many traffic signs

In Germany, research has revealed that too many traffic signs can become the *cause* of accidents. At first sight, this research doesn't seem to make any sense. Does it mean that traffic signs are a bad thing? Definitely not. But they are symbolic of secondary virtues. While a certain number of traffic signs helps reduce accidents, too many signs can have the opposite effect. The moment traffic signs distract drivers from primary virtues such as attentive driving or the ability to react quickly to unforeseen circumstances, driving becomes hazardous. Such an approach can kill people.

*In this graphic, the inner circle displays primary virtues (compassion, trustworthiness, acceptance); the outer circle, secondary virtues (fairness, honesty, politeness). While the three primary virtues are closely connected to each other, the secondary virtues can be performed without taking the other color segments into account.*

For me, this example has become a metaphor for many churches. According to the Barna Research Group, there is a considerably *higher* divorce rate in the United States among fundamentalist Christians (30%) than among non-Christians (23%). Again, at first sight these numbers don't seem to make any sense. It would be sad enough, but maybe somehow explainable, if the divorce rate among fundamentalists and "the world" were the same. But a remarkably *higher* rate among them signifies that though they formally emphasize family values, there must be specific characteristics among them that are *causing* marriages to fail. Upon closer inspection, however, we may discover that many of these values really belong to the secondary virtues category. The core problem: too many traffic signs. Other research has shown that people who have grown up in "teetotal" communities are, statistically, three times more likely to become alcoholics, than those who haven't. The problem? Too many traffic signs.

In order not to be misunderstood: The "traffic signs" in and of themselves are not the problem. It is (a) their exaggerated number and (b) the failure to root them in "primary virtues."

# Strengths and liabilities of different cultures

O ver the past eight years, I have had the privilege of spending more time out of Germany than in Germany; and the majority of that time I have been outside of the Western world. These extensive travels have helped me to appreciate the strengths of different cultures while at the same time giving me first-hand exposure to their potential liabilities.

The goal of Natural Church Development has never been to develop one specific church model, and then export it to the rest of the world. Rather, we have tried to learn from as many cultures as possible and to share those insights with as many cultures as possible. A globalized world offers unique learning experiences that were not available to us until recently.

### A "three-color look" at today's world

The graphic on page 45 portrays three cultural poles of today's world: the West, the East, and the South. I am well aware that typologies like this don't do justice to the rich diversity inside each of these cultural zones. Nevertheless, this diagram can help us see certain *tendencies* that are characteristic of the larger geographical areas.

*A globalized world offers unique learning experiences that were not available to us until recently.*

• The *Western world* (encompassing both North America and Europe; Australia is culturally related to the Western world as well, but distinctive in its geographic placement and cultural identity) has distinguished itself in its quest for truth. However, whenever this orientation has not been balanced by an equal insistence on justice and grace, an imperialistic mind-set has often been the result: "We must export the truth all over the world, even if it requires violence."

• The *Eastern world* (encompassing most of Asia) is very different. The various cultures in this part of the world have developed diverse forms of expressing politeness, honor, and respect that are virtually unknown in the Western world. Many of these cultures have learned to accept a veil of grace that shelters people, both literally and metaphorically. However, when this strength is not accompanied by a focus on truth and justice, there is the danger of hypocrisy.

• The *Southern world* (basically Latin America and Africa, but touching South-East Asia as well) represents a third cultural pole. It is no surprise that the topic of social justice, both inside and outside the Christian church, has its most prominent advocates in this part of the world. However, whenever the pursuit of social justice is not accompanied by an equally strong focus on truth and grace, there is danger of anarchy.

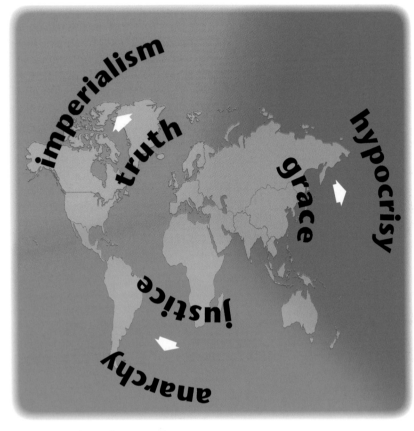

If we observe today's world, we can roughly distinguish three areas that share common cultural characteristics: the West, the East, and the South. Each of these three cultural zones has a specific strength (terms in the inner circle). However, if these strengths are isolated from each other (for instance, truth without justice and grace), problems occur. The three terms in the outer circle (imperialism, hypocrisy, and anarchy) describe the results.

## Understanding the paradigm

This scheme does *not* imply that every church in a given cultural zone is characterized by the color tendency mentioned above. We will find all three colors in each of these regions. What, then, can we learn from this way of looking at the world?

1.  The percentage of Christians within a certain cultural zone, who display the "main color" of their region, will be somewhat higher than in the other two zones. However, this by no means suggests that the number of people displaying the other colors won't be considerable as well.

2.  When it comes to the question of what a specific culture needs most, it's apparent that the key will be found outside of its own color segment. This insight presents quite an opportunity for our globalized world, were people smart enough to understand these dynamics. Since most of our politicians are far from this, at least we Christians can begin modeling how the world of tomorrow could function. In Natural Church Development, we are committed to this approach.

# Two different approaches in conflict

**W**hen the New Testament speaks of love, it usually uses the term *agape*. We will only be able to appreciate what *agape* means, if we understand the nature of God. The main thrust of *agape* as portrayed in the Bible suggests a love that is not stimulated by the person being loved (that would be characteristic of the secular-romantic notion of love); rather, it loves the other person because it *chooses* to love.

*Since God's love is in you, you can choose to think loving thoughts and do loving deeds.*

In New Testament times, like today, there were other concepts of love as well. When non-Christian Greeks spoke of love, they usually used the term *eros*. This word did not only refer to sexual desire. *Eros* is a general longing for something that one does not have, but ought to have or would like to have. It's a love stimulated by the person or object loved. *Eros* means, "I want you, I need you, I desire you, because I'm incomplete without you."

### The eros approach

The distinction between *eros* and *agape* can serve as a foundation for a typology that has far-reaching consequences. *Eros* depends on feelings that have been stimulated by the person being loved. This is the only way the person loving becomes capable of loving thoughts, which in turn lead to loving deeds. These dynamics can be represented as follows:

| Loving feelings | ▶ | Loving thoughts | ▶ | Loving deeds |

Most people's notion of love is based on the *eros* approach. Feelings come at the beginning of the process. Many Christians find it difficult to demonstrate love through loving deeds when it is not in keeping with their feelings. They believe that it would be hypocritical. Within the framework of the *eros* approach, this argument is perfectly logical. Without feelings it cannot work.

### The agape approach

The *agape* approach has a different starting point. Since *agape* is not stimulated by the person loved but by the person loving, it is not dependent on loving feelings to initiate the process. It begins with a *choice* to think loving thoughts. Any person who has experienced the love of God is capable of making this choice. Our loving thoughts enable us to perform loving deeds. While it cannot be guaranteed, these deeds very often have a positive effect on our feelings. The *agape* approach can be represented by the following diagram:

Note that this approach does *not* exclude our feelings. Yet they are not necessarily experienced at the beginning of the process. Most often, they come at the end. In other words, they follow our thoughts and our deeds. *Agape* means that you don't have to wait for loving feelings to emerge before you can love others. Since God's love is in you, you can choose to think loving thoughts and do loving deeds. And then you can lean back, relax, and marvel at the positive effect that your loving thoughts and deeds have on your feelings.

Only on the basis of the *agape* concept does Jesus' command to love our enemies make sense (Matt. 5:44). Actually, this command is a key to understanding what *agape* is all about. Jesus said, "If you love those who love you, what reward will you get? Are not even the tax collectors doing that? And if you greet only your brothers, what are you doing more than others? Do not even pagans do that?" (Matt. 5:46-47). There is nothing meritorious in the secular-romantic notion of love. If it works (i.e. if there are strong loving feelings), great! But if the feelings are missing, too bad! There will be nothing to carry you through times of emotional crisis. *Agape*, on the other hand, will enable you to love even in situations that begin with strong negative feelings.

### A first exercise

Take a moment to think of a person who is dependent on your love, but to whom it is difficult to express love. Now think through the practical effects that both the *eros* and the *agape* approaches would have on your relationship with that person. The following diagram is an example from my seminars. You may want to develop a similar diagram for the relationship you are working on.

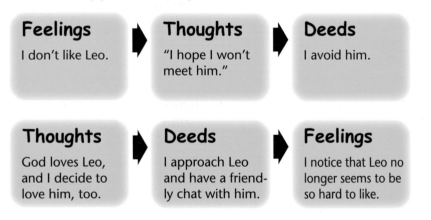

<table>
<tr><td>Chapter 1: Foundations</td></tr>
</table>

# Love can be learned

S ince our definition of love—even among Christians—has been shaped much more by the secular-romantic notion than by the biblical *agape* concept, many of us have a hard time understanding love as an art that can be learned.

Years ago, when I discovered the central importance of loving relationships for church development and tried to conduct seminars on love, I ran into the little problem that nobody would invite me to speak on the subject. However, since I was determined to gain experience in this area, I decided to take the initiative. The next seminar request I received, I suggested that we concentrate on the subject of love. The organizer did not seem opposed to the idea and asked, "How exactly should we title the seminar?" "How to increase your love-ability," I said spontaneously, since this was precisely what I wanted to explore in the seminar.

"That sounds far too methodical," the organizer said. "It almost suggests that love can be learned. Don't you have another suggestion?" I thought for a moment, and finally coined the title: "The historical dimension of the *agape* principle in the New Testament, comma, its meaning for practical ecclesiology today." The organizer was more than satisfied.

> Learning includes placing everything new that you hear in relationship with what you already know. It is an exhilarating experience, full of surprises.

### Opposition toward learning to love

How can we explain this strange reluctance to accept love as an art that can be learned? Anyone who wants to learn to drive would certainly not choose to attend a seminar titled: "The historical dimension of automobile transport, comma, its significance for modern traffic law." It would be far more adequate, unambiguous, and precise to offer "driving lessons." And if someone is interested in learning to cook, he or she would not be drawn to a seminar titled: "The dialectic tension between culinary ideal and economic reality in today's kitchens." They would prefer a simple, solid cooking class.

Whenever I use examples like these, I am always told that love cannot be compared with driving or cooking. I agree wholeheartedly. Love is indeed different from driving. But cooking is also different from driving. Nevertheless, there is *one* point that all three activities have in common (and in any comparison, we always have to focus on the common denominator). All of these activities require a lot of time and effort to learn. However, it seems that hardly anyone is prepared to admit that, in order to learn to love well, we need to invest just as much time and energy as we would to become a good driver or a good cook.

The truth of the matter is that if we didn't intuitively learn the principles of love in our families as we grew up, there is little probability that we will get a chance later on. Love is not on school curriculums. There are few universities that offer practical courses on love. Even our churches offer little in the way of practical support. No wonder most of us are just about as well equipped to love as an adventurer who sets out on a desert safari without a map or compass.

### Every second sermon: an exhortation to love

Given this reluctance to learn it might appear that little importance is placed on love in our churches. But that is just not true. Our institute did a survey among churches of various traditions that asked what percentage of the sermons the listeners were exhorted to become more loving. It was reported that 48% of all sermons included an appeal to love. This means that we are exhorted to love more in almost every other sermon we hear. On the basis of this result, we could get the impression that love is a top priority in our churches.

## Growing in love is not easy. It requires effort and hard work.

The shocker, however, is that when we asked the same group of Christians what practical opportunities were offered in their churches to learn the art of love, 77% said that in their church there was no such opportunity. Why is it that Christians are regularly exhorted to love, but are seldom offered practical training for growing in their ability to love?

Let me make a suggestion: For one year, let's do away with all general sermons on love, and set up weekly groups in which people can learn the art of love instead. I bet that this would be many times more effective than our present practice.

### Love is hard work

Growing in love is not easy. The Latin language had more than a dozen words to describe love, and the Romans were familiar with all of them. *Amor* and *caritas* are the best known of these terms. However, there was also a word that would probably come as a surprise to most of us: *studium*, which is the Latin root of the English word "study." Latin scholars tell us that this word expresses a particularly characteristic aspect of love.

Real "study" requires a lot of effort. It is hard work. Above all, it is a lifelong endeavor. We are always learning, even (or especially) when we are not sitting in a lecture, or a seminar, or reading a book. Learning includes placing everything new that you hear in relationship with what you already know. It is an exhilarating experience, full of surprises.

Some people are afraid of this process. For them, learning is something they unlearned when they finished school, or at least when they completed their vocational training. They are so glad it's over! But with this attitude, they are cheating themselves. Continually learning new things is one of the greatest adventures of life, as it constantly renews us. In a way, each new learning experience transforms us into a new person.

**Chapter 1: Foundations**

# Your personal growth process

W hen I conducted my first love seminar, I wanted to invite my fiancée (who, surprisingly, is now my wife) to attend. At that time, we lived about 150 miles apart, so we didn't see each other very often. I phoned her. "Brigitte," I said, "I have signed both of us up for a love seminar. Are you happy?"

I noticed that Brigitte was lost for words. I got the impression that she was inwardly jumping for joy, because she had not expected me to do such a thing. "You really want to take the time to attend a seminar like that with me?" she asked, almost unable to believe it.

"Of course," I said. "We're getting married in the not-too-distant future, so this subject is important for both of us." Brigitte was overjoyed, since she was not used to hearing me talk like that.

After a while, she asked, "Tell me, Christian, who is the speaker?" "Me," I said, with as much self-confidence as I was able to muster.

There was a strange silence at the other end of the line. "Oh," Brigitte finally said, her voice lacking its previous excitement. "I had hoped so much to learn something."

**A constant learning process**

Well, I am not a world champion in the art of loving, and people who spend a lot of time with me know this. But there is one thing that comforts me. Most of the participants in my seminars are just like me. "World champions" in the art of loving would hardly attend such a seminar.

*Deliberately concentrate on your own color deficiencies. Once you have discovered them, you will know what you have to do in order to grow in love.*

But people like me, who are conscious of their own short-comings, are willing to absorb anything that can help them along the way. I'm not ashamed of being who I am: a human being who is eager to learn. And in the past few years I have discovered that considerable growth is indeed possible.

**Eight practical suggestions**

As you turn to the practical exercises of the next chapters, keep the following points in mind:

*1. Develop your own growth process.*

The pages of this book have wide margins. As you work through its contents, "edit" them to fit you better. Use a pencil and a highlighter to make notes, jot down questions, and record your progress. Don't treat my text and graphics with too much respect. Leave your own mark on this book. After working with it for a while, your copy will be an original edition.

*2. Deliberately train different love muscles.*

Please note that the exercises provided in this book are not primarily targeted at ministering love to other people. Rather they are part of a training program that should *equip you* to minister love to other people better. This distinction is essential. There may be exercises in the training program that, at the moment you perform them, are not the best possible way of expressing God's love toward a specific person. But they are essential for *you*, to train all of your "love muscles," not just a specific set of them. And don't be surprised when you find exercises that seem to contradict each other. Your love muscles, metaphorically speaking, should eventually be able to move in all possible directions—even opposite directions—in order to release your full God-given potential.

*3. Don't get stuck at a purely intellectual level.*

> Could there be a better job description for a Christian small group to grow in love toward God, yourself, and other human beings?

The individual principles that you find in this book are meaningless if they are not applied to your life. Therefore, put the things that apply to you into practice, and do it immediately! You won't learn anything about the art of love until you practice your newly discovered skills. Total, real-life immersion is the best classroom for learning to love.

*4. Deliberately concentrate on your color deficiencies.*

The next chapter of this book will help you identify which of your love muscles most need a workout. Once you have discovered your weak points, you will know what you have to do in order to grow in love. Don't make the mistake of picking out just those exercises that you *like* most; rather, choose those that you *need* most. Is your self-control muscle flabby? No problem, it can be trained. Is your kindness muscle, your patience muscle, or your faithfulness muscle underdeveloped? Work it out for a number of weeks, and monitor your progress. You will be amazed how quickly you make progress once you begin focusing on one particular weakness rather than trying to grow in love "in general."

*5. Begin slowly.*

Don't set your sights too high. Always think about the next step—not about what you may do twenty years from now. For example, if you are particularly shy, you shouldn't force yourself to build new relationships with total strangers. You can save that for later. For now, just try to improve the quality of the relationships you already have.

*6. Leave your comfort zone.*

As we have mentioned before, you will only experience growth if you are willing to leave your comfort zone again and again. It's a pity, but a lot of Christians seem to expect a training course in love to stay within the narrow confines of their comfort zones. With that kind of attitude, it's absolutely impossible to discover new horizons, add new facets to your personality, or explore new ministry opportunities in your church. If you should find yourself feeling miserable while performing a certain exercise, take this as an indicator that training is taking place. You are growing, you are maturing, your emotions are indicating that God is working in your life. Just imagine what kind of person you will be when this training is complete: a person capable of communicating God's love appropriately in diverse situations.

*Don't get stuck at a purely intellectual level. You won't learn anything about the art of love if you don't apply your newly discovered skills.*

*7. Take your time.*

Love cannot be learned by reading a book. All of the exercises given here take time. You may want to read the book through quickly to get an overview of its contents. If you choose to do this, mark the exercises that you intend to do your second time through. The more time you spend training the different areas of justice, truth, and grace in your life, the greater your chances of becoming an increasingly loving person. And if you keep coming back to some of these exercises in the years ahead—so much the better.

*8. Join a group of Christians who are working through this book.*

Such a group may be an existing small group or a group set up specifically for the purpose of growing in love. In a small group context, learning processes can be much more intense. If you are already part of a small group, suggest the possibility of focusing together on the subject of love for a few weeks. If you aren't part of such a group consider joining one. Or start your own *3 Colors of Love* group. Make sure that each participant receives a copy of *The 3 Colors of Love*. Information about other support tools for such a group, including a handbook for small group leaders can be found at the end of this book.

Could there be a better job description for a Christian small group than to grow in love toward God, yourself, and other human beings inside and outside of your church?

# How to reflect God's love

*If loving means reflecting the light of God's love, we have to check, metaphorically speaking, whether or not there are any smudges on our "mirror" that need cleaning. That is exactly the focus of this chapter. It will help you identify your personal starting point in the process: those areas of your life in which your love most needs perfecting. To do this, we will have a closer look at love as the "fruit of the Spirit" (Galatians 5:22).*

# Fruit is visible

In my book, *Natural Church Development*, I point out the fact that, according to our international research, growing churches have a higher "love quotient" on average than stagnant or declining ones. While the average love quotient in growing churches is 56, it is only 47 in declining churches (these values are the so-called "T-values," with a mean value of 50).

> Growing churches have a higher love quotient on average than stagnant or declining ones.

The exact mathematical calculation of a love quotient is probably the most graphic indication that, in our endeavor to help churches grow, we should concentrate on the qualitative roots of growth. If quality is high, we no longer need to fret over quantity (worship attendance). All other things being equal, quantitative growth will happen "all by itself." For this reason, our Natural Church Development Partners around the world offer the NCD Survey, which gives churches the exact values for each of the eight quality characteristics of a healthy church, one of which is loving relationships. On the basis of this survey, churches can set qualitative goals and make action plans for how to improve their quality.

### What the love quotient measures

Of course, no scientific methodology in the world can measure love itself. What can be measured, however (and it can be measured well), are some of the practical expressions of love. How often do church members invite each other over for a meal or a cup of coffee? When believers are having problems, is there someone in their church with whom they feel free to pour out their hearts? How at home do people feel in their small groups? These items, and many more, are used to calculate a church's love quotient.

I must admit that, in contrast to many other Christians, I like the term "love quotient" very much, since it doesn't leave any room for a romantic, foggy, and thus unbiblical notion of love. The Bible repeatedly points out that love is more than a feeling. It speaks of love as "fruit" (Gal. 5:22). In Luke's gospel we read, "Each tree is recognized by its own fruit" (Luke 6:44). Fruit is not invisible. The Danish philosopher Søren Kierkegaard said that love itself is hidden. "However," he added, "this hidden life of love is known by its fruits, and love itself has an inborn need to be recognized by its fruits." In short, the widespread concept of "invisible fruit" is an unfruitful view.

### A little more romantic, please!

I often find that Christians react negatively to the very mention of the term "love quotient." I'm sure that most people would like my love seminars (and even me) better if I spoke about love in a more flowery, vague, ambiguous, and—some would say—poetic way.

In one of my seminars, I noticed that a participant looked mildly hostile as soon as I started to speak about the love quotient. During the break, I approached her and asked what had caused her negative feelings. She showed me a wonderful, copiously illustrated Christian book on love that she had brought along from home. On one page was written, "Love means seeing others with the eyes of Jesus," and if I remember correctly, the accompanying illustration was a sunset (it might also have been a rainbow or an apple tree). She said, "I find this much more convincing than your dreadful love quotient."

I agreed that the quote was wonderful, and then added that the goal of my seminar was to put such concepts into practice. At the beginning of the next session, I wrote the following on an overhead transparency, "Seeing others with the eyes of Jesus—10 practical steps." I wanted to set about drawing up practical action plans so that this wonderful concept could be put into practice in the following weeks. What does it mean to see others with the eyes of Jesus on Monday, Tuesday, Thursday? What does it mean for church life, our small groups, our families, our jobs? How does it relate to dealing with our opponents? What would be the consequences for politics? Very challenging questions indeed, loaded with practical relevance, potential conflicts, and emotion.

But after I had done this, the lady who had shown me this sentence protested again and looked even more angry than before. According to her, my suggestions were "far too technical," "not in tune with the essence of love", and above all, I was, in her eyes, "a terribly unpoetic human being." I had to ask myself: Is love really no more than the sort of nebulous feeling that runs up and down our spines when we look at an illustrated book of sunsets, rainbows, and apple trees? I don't doubt that experiencing this sort of romantic feeling might be more pleasant than working hard at increasing our capacity to love. But none of us should believe that those things with which we are most comfortable are necessarily more biblical.

**The fruit of love is visible. The widespread concept of invisible fruit is an unfruitful view.**

### Love must express itself in action

All three of the biblical authors that we have studied as models for justice, truth, and grace have, in one respect, exactly the same message. Whether you look at *James* ("Faith by itself, if it is not accompanied by action, is dead" —James 2:17), *John* ("Let us not love with words or tongue but with actions and in truth" —1 John 3:18), or *Paul* ("The only thing that counts is faith expressing itself through love" —Gal. 5:6), all of them insist on the necessity of putting the right knowledge into action.

My experience has been that those who struggle with the concept behind the term "love quotient" usually find applying the teachings of James, John and Paul difficult as well.

# Understanding the fruit of the Spirit

Galatians 5:22-23 is one of the classical biblical texts on the essence of love. In most translations, the text reads like this, "The fruit of the Spirit is love, joy, peace, patience, kindness, goodness, faithfulness, gentleness, and self-control." At first sight, the meaning looks very clear. Paul gives nine different terms to describe the fruit of the Spirit. One of these terms is "love," another is "joy," another, "peace," and so on. This is, by and large, the most common understanding of the text.

Upon closer observation, however, this interpretation doesn't seem to be consistent with what we learn throughout the Bible about the nature of love. It certainly makes sense to understand virtues like gentleness and faithfulness as distinct from each other; but to understand love as just one more of these virtues, on the same order as gentleness, faithfulness, kindness, and peace, doesn't seem to do it justice. Doesn't love, as it is described in the Bible, already contain all of these aspects?

**All Christians need to show the fruit of the Spirit.**

## A colon instead of a comma

Clarifying possibilities present themselves the moment we look at the Greek text. Ancient Greek didn't use punctuation marks of any kind, i.e. all of the punctuation that we find in our Bible translations (including Greek editions of the New Testament) are already interpretations. Look at the table at the bottom of this page. Instead of placing a comma after

*The table illustrates why Paul, in Galatians 5:22-23, might have used a singular verb ("the fruit ... is ...") followed by nine expressions. There is one fruit (love) with eight different aspects: joy, peace, patience, kindness, goodness, faithfulness, gentleness, and self-control.*

---

*Galatians 5:22-23 as we find it in most of our Bibles today (left Greek, right English):*

| | |
|---|---|
| ὁ δὲ καρπὸς τοῦ πνεύματός ἐστιν ἀγάπη, | But the fruit of the Spirit is love, |
| χαρὰ, εἰρήνη, μακροθυμία, χρηστότης, | joy, peace, patience, kindness, |
| ἀγαθωσύνη, πίστις, πραΰτης, ἐγκράτεια. | goodness, faithfulness, gentleness, self-control. |

---

*The original text, however, had no punctuation marks:*

| | |
|---|---|
| ὁ δὲ καρπὸς τοῦ πνεύματός ἐστιν ἀγάπη | But the fruit of the Spirit is love |
| χαρὰ εἰρήνη μακροθυμία χρηστότης | joy peace patience kindness |
| ἀγαθωσύνη πίστις πραΰτης ἐγκράτεια | goodness faithfulness gentleness self-control |

---

*A different way of punctuating this verse would be to put a colon after "love":*

| | |
|---|---|
| ὁ δὲ καρπὸς τοῦ πνεύματός ἐστιν ἀγάπη: | But the fruit of the Spirit is love: |
| χαρὰ, εἰρήνη, μακροθυμία, χρηστότης, | joy, peace, patience, kindness, |
| ἀγαθωσύνη, πίστις, πραΰτης, ἐγκράτεια. | goodness, faithfulness, gentleness, self-control. |

"love," we could just as easily place a colon. If we punctuate the text like this, it reads, "The fruit of the Spirit is love," followed by a colon, which would function the same as the English "i.e." Following the colon we find eight different expressions of love. In short, there aren't nine different fruits, one of which is love. Rather, there is one fruit, love, whose conceptual richness can be expressed with a collection of eight different terms. Such an understanding lends itself well to the all-encompassing nature of divine love as it is described in Scripture.

> As far as spiritual fruit is concerned, the following rule applies: Focus on your weakest areas.

### Gifts and fruit

It is important to distinguish carefully between the "gifts of the Spirit" and the "fruit of the Spirit." I believe it is misleading that some Bible translations subtitle 1 Corinthians 13, Paul's major teaching on love, "The greatest gift." Of course, we could understand love as a "gift," in the same way as the New Testament describes "eternal life" as a "gift" (Romans 6:23). But in *this* context, the use of the term "gift" in reference to love gives the impression that love is another spiritual gift of the kind that is described in 1 Corinthians 12. But that's not true.

Love is not a spiritual gift. It is the fruit of the Spirit. This distinction is far more than an academic game with words and concepts. It has far-reaching, practical consequences.

### Minimum factors and maximum factors

When dealing with spiritual gifts, the norm is that each Christian has only some of the many gifts that the Bible mentions. We can—and should—concentrate on the development and use of the gifts that God has given to us, allowing the gifts of other Christians to complement our own. For instance, if you have the gifts of service, hospitality, and evangelism, you should invest most of your energy in related ministries. And you should not feel guilty or inferior for not having the gifts of leadership, teaching, and counseling.

As far as spiritual gifts are concerned, the following rule applies: *Focus on your strengths rather than on your weaknesses.* If we were to apply NCD terminology, we would call it a "maximum factor strategy."

With the fruit of the Spirit, it's a different story. Every Christian is responsible for growing in love, and is expected to show the fruit of the Spirit in his or her life. As far as the fruit of the Spirit is concerned, we cannot pick out some elements and set others aside. Rather, we must strive to express *all* aspects of this fruit in our lives: joy, peace, patience, kindness, goodness, faithfulness, gentleness, and self-control. Our growth in love is hindered, first of all, by our greatest weakness.

As far as spiritual fruit is concerned, this rule applies: *Focus especially on your weakest areas.* Again, translated into the technical language of Natural Church Development, this would be a "minimum factor strategy."

### So... Which area should I work on?

Let me give you an example. When I took our *Fruit of the Spirit Test* for the first time, I identified "self-control" as my primary weakness. If I—wrongly—were to have applied the "maximum factor" strategy to this result, I could have said, "What's the problem? My greatest strength is the fruit of joy. Let me go on being happy, invest even more in the area of joy, and let others practice more self-discipline in their lives." Such an approach would be biblically, spiritually, and psychologically disastrous—both for myself and for the people I relate to.

When dealing with the fruit of the Spirit, a "minimum factor" strategy applies. Because my main weakness was self-control, I needed to focus primarily on that area. When I recently re-did the *Fruit of the Spirit Test* while preparing this book, I was encouraged to discover that self-control is no longer my "minimum fruit." My training efforts have taken effect!

### The spiritual color wheel

In the diagram on the right (page 59), love is placed at the very center. The eight terms that characterize love as the fruit of the Spirit are distributed around the black wheel, each one with a specific affinity to one or two of the three color areas: justice, truth, and grace. Some terms can be directly related to one of these three dimensions; others are placed on the border between two color areas.

At first sight, artificial fruit looks as beautiful as real fruit. But take one bite, and the wax in your teeth will remind you not to try that again.

Outside of the color wheel you find three different aspects of "darkness": deception, mercilessness, and injustice (see page 26). Let's imagine that you have identified a personal tendency toward one of these areas. One way to deal with this could be to avoid the negative actions, thoughts, or habits that are at the root of injustice, mercilessness, or deception. However, the spiritual color wheel suggests an alternate way of dealing with areas of darkness in your life. Rather than focusing on reforming the darkness, focus on nurturing those expressions of love that you find on the *opposite side* of the color wheel.

Do you want to fight the darkness of mercilessness? Let the lights of kindness and gentleness shine! Is the darkness of injustice your problem? Focus on patience, goodness, and peace! Is deception your problem area? Work on faithfulness and self-control! In any change process it is important to focus on the patterns you want to introduce, not on the ones you want to avoid. As someone once wisely said, "Don't curse the darkness. Light a candle."

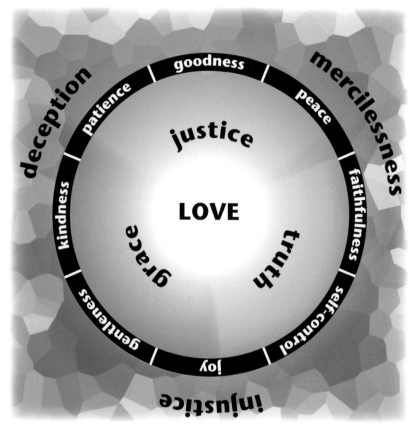

*In this color wheel, the fruit of the Spirit (Gal. 5:22-23) is related to the three areas of justice, truth, and grace. Whereas some terms can clearly be assigned to one of the three colors (goodness, faithfulness, self-control, gentleness, kindness), there are others that cover two color segments rather than one (patience, peace, joy).*

### Natural and artificial fruit

Note that not everything that looks like patience, goodness, peace etc. is by necessity a "spiritual fruit." There is artificial fruit that may look as beautiful as real fruit at first sight. But take one bite, and the wax in your teeth will remind you not to try that again.

To state this without the metaphor: One could, in a seminar, train others to smile and laugh in order to express joy, even if those expressions are not rooted in love. You could apply excellent listening techniques and give the impression of patience even if it has nothing to do with spiritual fruit. You could show acts of kindness without living in the dimension of grace and thus reflecting God's love. The same holds true for all of the other expressions of the fruit of the Spirit as well.

Some people are so fascinated by artificial fruit that they consider it superior to natural fruit. You don't have to plant it, water it, nurture it. It's true: Artificial fruit is far easier to care for than natural fruit. But once you have experienced the sweet taste of real fruit that you have grown, you realize that all of your efforts were well worth while.

# 1 Corinthians 13 and the spiritual color wheel

Paul made it crystal clear to the Christians in Corinth that even the most committed life is worth nothing without the fruit of the Spirit. In 1 Corinthians 13 he told them that they could have all knowledge (which clearly relates to the dimension of truth), give all their possessions to the poor (the dimension of justice) and even give their own lives away (the dimension of grace)—but without love all of this would be in vain. Once again, we are dealing with the distinction between primary and secondary virtues (see pages 41-43).

> Each of us should write our own version of 1 Corinthians 13:1 to test how strongly our lives are driven by authentic love.

### Your own version of 1 Corinthians 13:1

Paul starts his famous chapter on love with the words, "If I speak in the tongues of men and of angels, but have not love, I am only a resounding gong or a clanging cymbal" (1 Cor. 13:1). It would be beneficial for you to formulate your own version of this verse, reflecting your personal situation. If you are a preacher, for instance, you could write, "If I got into the pulpit Sunday after Sunday and preached a splendid sermon and the church were packed to the last seat, yet I had no love for the people in the pews—it would be better for me to keep my mouth shut."

If I had to formulate my own version of this verse, I would write, "If I had all the church growth knowledge in the world and knew all the secrets of Natural Church Development, if I could calculate the love quotient of a church to two decimal places and spent twelve months of the year travelling to the remotest places of the earth in order to pass on this knowledge—if my motive were anything else than love for the people I deal with, I would be nothing more than a boring technocrat." Each of us should write our own versions of this verse to test how strongly our lives are driven by love. What would your version say?

### How love expresses itself

In the midst of this famous chapter, Paul gives a precise characterization of how love expresses itself: "Love is patient, love is kind. It does not envy, it does not boast, it is not proud. It is not rude, it is not self-seeking, it is not easily angered, it keeps no record of wrongs. Love does not delight in evil but rejoices with the truth. It always protects, always trusts, always hopes, always perseveres. Love never fails" (1 Cor. 13:4-8). If you were searching world literature for a precise, encompassing, helpful, and relevant description of love—that is divinely inspired at that—here you have it.

In the diagram on page 61, I have related the description of love in 1 Corinthians 13 to the eight terms that Paul has introduced in Galatians 5:22-23 to describe the fruit of the Spirit. It's amazing how well these two passages, written in two different situations for two different audiences, compare.

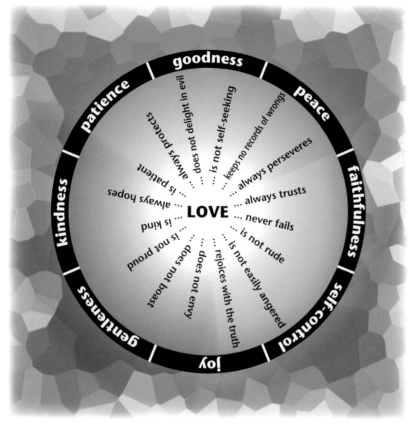

*Whether Paul writes about the fruit of the Spirit (as in Galatians 5:22-23) or presents an abundance of characteristics that constitute love (as in 1 Corinthians 13), he is constantly speaking about the same topic, just using different points of reference. If we place the text of 1 Corinthians 13 into our spiritual color wheel, each of the characteristics of love can be related to the fruit of the Spirit of Galatians 5:22-23.*

## Four in one

In the course of this book, we have introduced four biblical paradigms that speak of love. The diagram above shows how all of them inter-relate:

1. We built our whole approach on the biblical premise that *God is love* and therefore placed "love" at the very center of the diagram.

2. We investigated *three dimensions of God's love* (justice, truth, and grace) and represented them in our diagram by the colors green, red, and blue.

3. We studied Paul's teaching on love as the *fruit of the Spirit* and placed the eight expressions of this fruit on the black wheel of our diagram.

4. We made reference to *1 Corinthians 13* and integrated those descriptions of love as the spokes of our wheel.

These are four different paradigms—each of them addressing the exact same topic through a different looking glass. In the end, it's not really four paradigms, but one: the biblical paradigm of love. I have developed the "spiritual color wheel" to help us see this spiritual reality in context.

**Chapter 2: Your starting point**

# The Fruit of the Spirit Test

**Before you begin the test, just a few words of explanation:**

**1** Read through the following 64 statements and place an "X" on the answer that is *most applicable* to you. Answer as spontaneously as possible thinking primarily of recent experiences. Be honest with yourself. Only then will you get helpful results.

Would you like to identify your growth areas? Take 30 minutes to fill out the following questionnaire.

**2** Once you have answered all of the questions, tear out the evaluation sheet (pages 67-68) and follow the instructions given there. The results will bring to light which of the eight terms in Galatians 5:22-23 are most developed in your life, and which are least developed.

**3** Page 69 relates your results to the three areas of justice, truth, and grace. It will help you identify which of the color segments you should most focus on as you work on the practical exercises in chapter 3.

**4** I would be grateful if you would send me your completed evaluation sheet (page 67) or a copy of it (care of the publisher whose address appears on page 6 of this book). This feedback will help us with our ongoing research. Send this form with or without your name—the processing will be done anonymously anyway. Please include the following information in the margin of page 67: (a) your age, (b) your gender, (c) the denomination of your church, and (d) the name of your country.

**5** When you have completed these steps, turn to page 70 to have a closer look at those expressions of the fruit of the Spirit that have been identified as least developed in your life. It may also be worthwhile to study those areas that are already strongly developed.

**And now—enjoy the exercise!**

# It has...

# been my experience that...

| | very often | often | sometimes | rarely | never | been my experience that... |
|---|---|---|---|---|---|---|
| **1** | | | | | | ... I have responded with understanding when someone has done something wrong. |
| **2** | | | | | | ... others have been encouraged by my positive attitude toward life. |
| **3** | | | | | | ... I have played a constructive role in settling conflicts. |
| **4** | | | | | | ... people tell me that I am trustworthy. |
| **5** | | | | | | ... others have taken their cue from me in matters of moral conduct. |
| **6** | | | | | | ... my presence has encouraged other people. |
| **7** | | | | | | ... I have found it easy to restrain myself from overindulgence in things I enjoy. |
| **8** | | | | | | ... I have tended to see the positive side of other people. |
| **9** | | | | | | ... setbacks haven't stopped me from pursuing what I believed was right. |
| **10** | | | | | | ... others were encouraged as a result of being with me. |
| **11** | | | | | | ... I could bring harmony to a group of people. |
| **12** | | | | | | ... others have benefitted from my financial support. |
| **13** | | | | | | ... I have worked for the establishment of God's standards even in hostile environments. |
| **14** | | | | | | ... others have told me that they feel at home with me. |
| **15** | | | | | | ... others have complimented me for the way I organize my life. |
| **16** | | | | | | ... that I pointed out someone's virtues, when others were critical of them. |
| | 4 | 3 | 2 | 1 | 0 | |

# I...

| | very often | often | sometimes | rarely | never | tend to... |
|---|---|---|---|---|---|---|
| **17** | | | | | | ... get restless if I am confined to bed because I am sick. |
| **18** | | | | | | ... feel dejected when I am in a difficult situation. |
| **19** | | | | | | ... panic quickly. |
| **20** | | | | | | ... be skeptical of other people. |
| **21** | | | | | | ... turn a blind eye to sins other Christians commit that are also a temptation for me. |
| **22** | | | | | | ... notice the faults of others. |
| **23** | | | | | | ... lose control easily. |
| **24** | | | | | | ... get angry when other people make mistakes. |
| **25** | | | | | | ... get uptight if I have to wait in line. |
| **26** | | | | | | ... get depressed easily. |
| **27** | | | | | | ... create conflicts. |
| **28** | | | | | | ... fail to fulfill my commitments on time. |
| **29** | | | | | | ... treat wealthy or well-known people with more respect than others. |
| **30** | | | | | | ... see other people with critical eyes. |
| **31** | | | | | | ... lose balance in my life. |
| **32** | | | | | | ... be rude to others. |
| | 0 | 1 | 2 | 3 | 4 | |

# The following statement applies to me:

| | very much | to a large extent | moderately | slightly | not at all | |
|---|---|---|---|---|---|---|
| **33** | | | | | | I don't give up when harsh setbacks occur. |
| **34** | | | | | | I have a good sense of humor and enjoy a hearty laugh. |
| **35** | | | | | | I try to promote social justice in my area of responsibility. |
| **36** | | | | | | My friends can rely on me. |
| **37** | | | | | | "Holiness" is one of the highest values in my life. |
| **38** | | | | | | I like to make other people's lives more pleasant by taking care of the small details of life. |
| **39** | | | | | | My personal life is marked by discipline and order. |
| **40** | | | | | | I find it easy to accept criticism. |
| **41** | | | | | | People have told me that my life is characterized by perseverance. |
| **42** | | | | | | Discovering truth is an uplifting experience for me. |
| **43** | | | | | | I enjoy fostering reconciliation between people. |
| **44** | | | | | | It is important for me to stick to God's standards even when other people disregard them. |
| **45** | | | | | | I stand up for the rights of the poor. |
| **46** | | | | | | I tend to see needs that others overlook. |
| **47** | | | | | | My spiritual life is characterized by discipline. |
| **48** | | | | | | It is easy for me to accept people as they are. |
| | 4 | 3 | 2 | 1 | 0 | |

# I find it...

| | very easy | easy | neither easy nor hard | fairly difficult | very difficult | |
|---|---|---|---|---|---|---|
| **49** | | | | | | ... to grant others the necessary time to mature. |
| **50** | | | | | | ... to be happy in the midst of unfavorable circumstances. |
| **51** | | | | | | ... to take the first step toward reconciliation when I have had an argument with someone. |
| **52** | | | | | | ... to do exactly what I have promised. |
| **53** | | | | | | ... to point out to people things that are not right in their lives. |
| **54** | | | | | | ... to minister to people even if I cannot expect anything in return. |
| **55** | | | | | | ... to keep my emotions in check. |
| **56** | | | | | | ... to remain calm even in critical situations. |
| **57** | | | | | | ... to accept the imperfections of others. |
| **58** | | | | | | ... to radiate a positive spirit among negative people. |
| **59** | | | | | | ... to be generous with other people. |
| **60** | | | | | | ... to stick to the truth. |
| **61** | | | | | | ... to treat both the poor and the wealthy with the same respect. |
| **62** | | | | | | ... to be friendly to people who are not very friendly to me. |
| **63** | | | | | | ... to stick to rules. |
| **64** | | | | | | ... to forgive others. |
| | 4 | 3 | 2 | 1 | 0 | |

# How to evaluate the Fruit of the Spirit Test

**Have you answered all of the questions? Then you can begin with the evaluation. It is quite simple if you follow the five steps that are explained below:**

## Step 1: Tear out the page

Remove this evaluation sheet by tearing along the perforation. This will make the next step more convenient for you.

## Step 2: Collect the raw data

Using the following scoring grid, enter the numbers (0-4) that correspond to your answers on the questionnaire (p. 63-66). These numbers are found at the bottom of each column.

**Please note that the order of these numbers at the bottom of each page changes on questions 17 through 32.**

| | | | | | | | | Total | Name of fruit |
|---|---|---|---|---|---|---|---|---|---|
| 1 | 9 | 17 | 25 | 33 | 41 | 49 | 57 | | **Patience** |
| 2 | 10 | 18 | 26 | 34 | 42 | 50 | 58 | | **Joy** |
| 3 | 11 | 19 | 27 | 35 | 43 | 51 | 59 | | **Peace** |
| 4 | 12 | 20 | 28 | 36 | 44 | 52 | 60 | | **Faithfulness** |
| 5 | 13 | 21 | 29 | 37 | 45 | 53 | 61 | | **Goodness** |
| 6 | 14 | 22 | 30 | 38 | 46 | 54 | 62 | | **Kindness** |
| 7 | 15 | 23 | 31 | 39 | 47 | 55 | 63 | | **Self-control** |
| 8 | 16 | 24 | 32 | 40 | 48 | 56 | 64 | | **Gentleness** |

Now add up the eight numbers in every row of the table. Write the result for each row in the *Total* field. This will give you a "raw value" for each item.

Note that these values do not represent the results of the *Fruit of the Spirit Test*. To find out which fruit is most strongly developed in your life—and which one most needs perfecting—you need to transfer the raw data calculated above into the "normation table" found on page 68. The scientific normation has been developed by our institute on the basis of inter-denominational sample groups and is different for every language edition of this book.

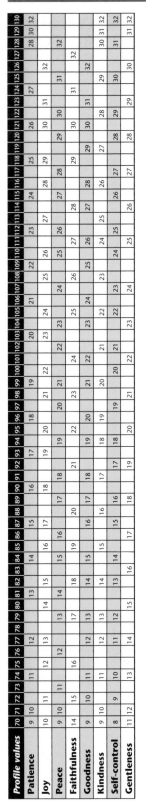

## How to evaluate the *Fruit of the Spirit Test* (continued)

### Step 3: Transfer the raw data to the normation table

After completing the scoring grid (step 2), transfer the totals for each fruit onto the normation table to the left. For each item, mark the number yielded by the scoring grid. For example, if the scoring grid shows a total of 27 for *Patience,* you should mark the number 27 in the normation table for the row labeled *Patience*. If the corresponding number does not appear, simply mark the next highest number.

### Step 4: View the results

The normation table now shows you which fruit has the highest value, and which one the lowest (see *profile values* in the black row). Write the name of each fruit into the table below, starting with the one that has the highest profile value, and ending with the one that has the lowest. Write the profile value of each one into the right column of the table.

### Step 5: Evaluate the results and take action

When interpreting your personal results, keep the following in mind:

a. The aspects of love that rank highest are already relatively strongly developed in your life. Look for ways to practice them more creatively than you have before.

b. When it comes to growing your spiritual fruit, you should first focus on those areas that have the lowest profile values (see pages 57-58).

c. Remember that it is helpful not to treat the individual items in isolation, but to think of them in relation to the three color areas that stand for justice, truth, and grace (see diagram on page 59). The next page will help you do this.

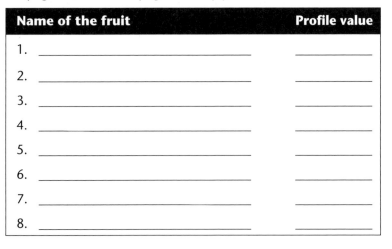

| Name of the fruit | Profile value |
| --- | --- |
| 1. | |
| 2. | |
| 3. | |
| 4. | |
| 5. | |
| 6. | |
| 7. | |
| 8. | |

# Which color area do you have to address?

Threlates them to the spiritual color wheel that has been described on page 59 (see instructions below).he following table takes your *Fruit of the Spirit Test* results and

| | Column A:<br>*Insert Profile Values* | Column B:<br>*Calculate* | Column C:<br>*Write down results* | Column D:<br>*Add up column C values* | | |
|---|---|---|---|---|---|---|
| Patience | | ÷ 10 = | x 8 = | | | |
| Goodness | | ÷ 10 = | x11 = | | } | Justice |
| Peace | | ÷ 10 = | x 8 = | | | |
| Peace | | ÷ 10 = | x 2 = | | | |
| Faithfulness | | | | | } | Truth |
| Self-control | | | | | | |
| Joy | | ÷ 2 | = | | | |
| Joy | | ÷ 2 | = | | | |
| Gentleness | | | | | } | Grace |
| Kindness | | | | | | |
| Patience | | ÷ 10 = | x 2 = | | | |

**Column A:** Write down the profile value for each spiritual fruit (see table on page 68). For some items (patience, peace, joy) the value will have to be entered twice, since they cover two color areas.

**Columns B and C:** For some rows of column B, you will have to do a small mathematical calculation. Write the results into column C. In those rows that don't require any calculation (faithfulness, self-control, gentleness, kindness), transfer the values of column A to column C.

**Column D:** Add up the figures of column C for each of the three color groupings. Write the results into column D. The bar with the highest value shows your strongest color, the bar with the lowest value your weakest color. In the practical exercises of chapter 3, you should focus on the color area that is currently your weakest.

### Selecting the most helpful exercises

Here you can see which exercises address each color area:

**Justice:** "Wear other people's glasses" (exercise 3), "Make yourself vulnerable" (exercise 6), "Be transparent" (exercise 8), "Have a meal together" (exercise 12).

**Truth:** "Love yourself" (exercise 2), "Put an end to spiritual hypocrisy" (exercise 4), "Learn to trust" (exercise 5), "Use your humor" (exercise 11).

**Grace:** "Fill up with God's love" (exercise 1), "Dare to forgive" (exercise 7), "Train active listening" (exercise 9), "Surprise with gifts" (exercise 10).

*The spiritual color wheel (see page 59) relates the fruit of the Spirit to the areas of justice, truth, and grace.*

**Chapter 2:
Your starting
point**

# What do the individual terms mean?

Note that the biblical meaning of some terms differs considerably from our everyday usage.

The following eight pages will help you gain a better understanding of what the different terms in Galatians 5:22-23 mean. Strictly speaking, we should refer to each of the eight terms as "expressions of the fruit of the Spirit," as we have seen before (pages 56-57). In order to avoid overly complicated language, however, throughout the remainder of the book we will refer to the individual expressions as "fruit" as well. This is both in line with other biblical usages of the term "fruit" (where it serves as a metaphor for a plethora of different expressions) and with its literal, non-metaphorical meaning: While all of the apples (in their entirety) on a tree are labeled "the fruit of this tree," we can also use this term for any of the individual apples.

You should start by studying the fruit that is least developed in your life at present. Each of the following pages begins with a short description of your situation (based on the assumption that this is, so to speak, your "minimum fruit"), followed by a suggestion of the direction in which you need to grow. After this introduction, you will find the following information:

## Understanding the term

Here I explain the biblical meaning of the respective fruit, usually with reference to the Greek term that is used in the New Testament. Please note that the biblical meaning of some terms differs considerably from our common usage today. Looking into the original root of the word can help you develop a genuinely biblical understanding of the different ways that love can be expressed.

## Color segment

This passage refers to the spiritual color wheel that was introduced on page 59. Each fruit is related to one (or two) of the three colors that we have used to represent justice, truth, and grace. The text explains why the fruit in question has been placed at that precise position on the color wheel. This is also illustrated by the heart symbol that you find on each page.

## Key Bible passage

For each fruit, I have selected one Bible passage that describes the essence of that fruit. These verses serve as the biblical paradigm behind the term in question.

## For further study

Under this heading I have selected additional New Testament texts that will give you an even better understanding of the term in question. In this list, I have not included those texts that have already been mentioned. When dealing with a specific fruit, make sure to study each of these verses in context.

# The fruit of patience: Enduring love

I f patience is your current weakness, you tend to expect results too quickly, which negatively affects both your relationship with yourself and with others. You will mature in love as you learn to give yourself and others time to grow naturally, which includes making mistakes and learning from them.

### Understanding the term

The Greek word *makrothymia* contemplates a persistence that is not easily put off by unfavorable circumstances. It is based on the patience of God, which never gives up on anyone.

Patience must not be confused with fatalism, i.e. simply accepting things as they are. On the contrary, patience, as described in the Bible, is active. It is a perseverance that works toward seeing God's will become reality. In this process, however, it has an eye for the right timing. In the New Testament, patience is often mentioned in close relationship to kindness and gentleness (as has also been done in our color wheel).

Literally, *makrothymia* means holding back the *thymos*, anger, for a long time. It is the opposite of *oxythymia,* violent anger. People who display patience are able to combine determination and mercy.

> Patience must not be confused with fatalism. Rather, it is a perseverance that combines determination with mercy.

### Color segment

On the spiritual color wheel (page 59), patience has been placed in the justice segment (green), slightly overlapping with grace (blue). The dimension of grace that is contained in patience is urgently needed when people are striving for justice.

### Key Bible passage: James 5:7-9

"Be patient, then, brothers, until the Lord's coming. See how the farmer waits for the land to yield its valuable crop and how patient he is for the autumn and spring rains. You too, be patient and stand firm, because the Lord's coming is near. Don't grumble against each other, brothers, or you will be judged."

### For further study

Matthew 18:21-35; Romans 9:22-23; 1 Corinthians 13:4; Colossians 3:12-14; 1 Thessalonians 5:14-15; 2 Timothy 3:10-12; 2 Timothy 4:1-8; Hebrews 6:10-20; James 1:2-4; James 5:7-12; 2 Peter 3:4-16

# The fruit of joy:
# Rejoicing love

**I**f joy is your weakness, it would encourage both you and others if you could be more enthusiastic about the Lord and the ministry he has given you. You need to learn not to let your moods be so influenced by your environment.

### Understanding the term

The Greek term *chara* refers to a happiness that is based on the "joy of the Lord," and is therefore independent of the situation you happen to be in. Joy has nothing to do with a hedonistic striving after fun. It's more of a "happiness in" than a "happiness about." It doesn't ignore the sorrows and pains of life. In fact, the Bible frequently emphasizes that we can have joy in the midst of suffering.

> Joy is a happiness that is based on the "joy of the Lord." Therefore it is independent of the situation you happen to be in.

However, biblical joy should not be confused with the Stoic ideal of an emotionless state of being. In both the Old and the New Testaments, joy is definitely a term that is loaded with emotion. The Gospels teach us with the brightest colors what joy is all about. The more this fruit grows, the better we will be able to share the joy that we have experienced, with others.

The term *chara* is closely related to the New Testament term for grace, *charis.* In effect, we can view the whole gospel as a "word of joy." Luke in particular makes joy the underlying theme of his gospel.

### Color segment

Joy is as much an expression of truth (see 1 Cor. 13:6) as of grace (see above). Therefore we have placed it on our spiritual color wheel (page 59) between the red and blue color segments.

### Key Bible passage: Luke 10:17-20

"The seventy-two returned with joy and said, 'Lord, even the demons submit to us in your name.' He replied, 'I saw Satan fall like lightning from heaven. I have given you authority to trample on snakes and scorpions and to overcome all the power of the enemy; nothing will harm you. However, do not rejoice that the spirits submit to you, but rejoice that your names are written in heaven.'"

### For further study

John 15:9-11; Acts 5:41-42; Romans 14:17; Philippians 4:1-4; Colossians 1:24; Hebrews 10:34; James 1:2

# The fruit of peace: Reconciling love

I f peace is your current weakness, you should deliberately strive for reconciliation in the relationships around you. However, it may well be that you have to work on improving your own primary relationships before seeking to bring about reconciliation between others.

### Understanding the term

In the New Testament, the Greek term *eirene* in most cases acquires nuances from the Hebrew word *shalom,* which is far wider in scope. It includes both the state of being reconciled with God and one's wholeness in all aspects of life, from which peace with others flows.

It is no accident that the Bible begins and ends with the great vision of *shalom.* In the creation narrative, God brings order and harmony out of chaos. In the book of Revelation, people from all nations form a loving community in "the holy city, the new Jerusalem" (Rev. 21).

In Psalm 85:10 *shalom* is placed in the midst of our three key terms for understanding love: justice, truth, and grace. "Grace and truth meet together; justice and peace kiss each other." In Matthew 5:9 Jesus blesses the peacemakers and promises them that they will be called "sons of God."

### Color segment

Peace is an expression of justice (see Isa. 32:17), but it has a tendency toward truth as well. Therefore, on our spiritual color wheel (page 59), we have placed it inside the green segment, bordering the red segment.

> Peace, in the biblical sense, contemplates a far broader reality than our common usage of the English term. It aims at the well-being of an individual or community in all aspects of life.

### Key Bible passage: Romans 12:16-18

"Live in harmony with one another. Do not be proud, but be willing to associate with people of low position. Do not be conceited. Do not repay anyone evil for evil. Be careful to do what is right in the eyes of everybody. If it is possible, as far as it depends on you, live at peace with everyone."

### For further study

Mark 9:50; John 14:27; Romans 5:1-2; 2 Corinthians 13:11; Ephesians 2:14-17; Philippians 4:7; Hebrews 12:11-15; James 3:18

# The fruit of faithfulness: Reliable love

**Faithfulness means practicing the "good stewardship" that Jesus expects of his disciples.**

If faithfulness should be your weakest area, you could make great progress in your growth process by learning to be more reliable in terms of your commitments. This would make you more trustworthy in the eyes of other people.

### Understanding the term

The word for "faithfulness" in the Greek text, *pistis,* is the same word that is otherwise often translated as "faith." In the New Testament, faithfulness includes reliability and trustworthiness—you trust others, and, in turn, earn their trust. The parable of the talents (Matt. 25:14-30) is a prime example of the sort of faithful stewardship that God expects of us.

In the Bible, faithfulness is always a relational term, it is concerned with commitments toward other people. It's unfaithful not to use the gifts that God has given us (Luke 19:20-22). In the same way, it can be unfaithful to commit ourselves to so many tasks that we cannot follow through adequately. Good stewardship implies the ability to say "no."

As we have seen before (page 32), in the Old Testament "faithfulness" is another translation of the Hebrew word for "truth." The reliability embodied by this term is at the core of a genuinely biblical concept of truth.

### Color segment

Since "faithfulness" and "truth" are synonyms in the Old Testament, we have placed faithfulness at the center of the red segment.

### Key Bible passage: Luke 16:10-12

"Whoever can be trusted with very little can also be trusted with much, and whoever is dishonest with very little will also be dishonest with much. So if you have not been trustworthy in handling worldly wealth, who will trust you with true riches? And if you have not been trustworthy with someone else's property, who will give you property of your own?"

### For further study

Luke 12:42-48; Luke 16:1-8; Romans 4:17-20; 1 Corinthians 4:1-2; 2 Timothy 2:13; Hebrews 10:23

# The fruit of goodness: Correcting love

I f goodness is currently a weakness for you, you definitely could be "harder" on yourself and others. As far as God's standards are concerned, a certain amount of strictness can well reflect a spirit of love.

## Understanding the term

The English word "goodness" can portray a false understanding of the term, since we tend to think of it as "mildness." The Greek term, *agathosyne,* means something very different.

Just as *dikaiosyne* (justice) is the noun derived from the adjective *dikaios* (just), *agathosyne* is the noun derived from the adjective *agathos* (good). In other words, the term means striving for the standards that God has defined as "good." It is an attitude of opposition to all forms of evil—in our own lives as well as in the lives of others.

Goodness, in the biblical sense, is an expression of God's correcting love. It identifies an evil situation and tries to bring about change. Jesus' cleansing of the temple (see passage below), is a prime example of *agathosyne* in action.

> Goodness, in Greek, has a very different meaning from our present use of the term. It means striving for the standards that God has defined as good.

## Color segment

The fruit of goodness (understood in the biblical sense) is an expression of justice. We have therefore placed it at the center of the green segment.

## Key Bible passage: Mark 11:15-17

"On reaching Jerusalem, Jesus entered the temple area and began driving out those who were buying and selling there. He overturned the tables of the money changers and the benches of those selling doves, and would not allow anyone to carry merchandise through the temple courts. And as he taught them, he said, 'Is it not written: 'My house will be called a house of prayer for all nations'? But you have made it a den of robbers.'"

## For further study

Matthew 5:17-20; Mark 10:18; Romans 12:2; Romans 15:14; Ephesians 5:1-9; 2 Thessalonians 1:6-12

# The fruit of kindness: Amiable love

I f kindness is lacking in your life, you should try to project a more winsome attitude. It's especially important that you develop an eye for the little things that bring joy to other people's lives.

### Understanding the term

Kindness—in Greek *chrestotes*—can express itself through many simple details of life and relationships: being interested in others, giving gifts, showing attention, listening to people, remembering names, etc.

> Kindness radiates an atmosphere that is at the very center of the term "grace." It expresses itself in the many small details of life.

Kindness radiates an atmosphere that is at the very center of the term "grace." As this fruit grows in the life of people, they will be able to radiate God's grace even without using words.

When Paul integrated kindness into his description of love, he was doing more than merely borrowing the term from similar lists of virtues that were widespread at that time. Rather, he was responding to God's kindness, which he had experienced so overwhelmingly in his own life (Rom. 11:22).

### Color segment

Since kindness expresses an "atmosphere of grace," we have placed it at the center of the blue segment.

### Key Bible passage: Luke 10:30-35

"A man was going down from Jerusalem to Jericho, when he fell into the hands of robbers. They stripped him of his clothes, beat him and went away, leaving him half dead. A priest happened to be going down the same road, and when he saw the man, he passed by on the other side. So too, a Levite, when he came to the place and saw him, passed by on the other side. But a Samaritan, as he traveled, came where the man was; and when he saw him, he took pity on him. He went to him and bandaged his wounds, pouring on oil and wine. Then he put the man on his own donkey, took him to an inn and took care of him. The next day he took out two silver coins and gave them to the innkeeper. 'Look after him,' he said, 'and when I return, I will reimburse you for any extra expense you may have.'"

### For further study

2 Corinthians 6:6; Ephesians 2:4-7; Ephesians 4:29-32; Colossians 3: 12-14; Titus 3:4-8

# The fruit of self-control: Disciplined love

I f self-control should be a weakness for you, the pursuit of greater consistency in your personal life might be the most important step you can take toward becoming a more loving person. If you paid more attention to discipline, it would benefit both you and others.

### Understanding the term

The Greek word *egkrateia* means sobriety, restraint, and moderation in all areas of life. It includes far more than is implied by the term "temperance," which is used in some of the older translations (even if this is one variety of self-control). The basic meaning of self-control is "having power over yourself."

The term is semantically related to the word *askeo*, from which our word "ascetic" stems. The literal meaning of *askeo* is simply *train*. Training includes abstaining from many things in order to reach a specific goal (1 Cor. 9:24-27).

Self-control is not an end in itself, even if throughout church history many people have understood it that way. Rather, its goal is to serve other people better.

> Self-control means sobriety and moderation in all areas of life. It's always targeted at achieving a specific goal.

### Color segment

Self-control is strongly related to the steadfastness and reliability that characterizes the red color segment as a whole.

### Key Bible passage: 1 Corinthians 9:24-27

"Do you not know that in a race all the runners run, but only one gets the prize? Run in such a way as to get the prize. Everyone who competes in the games goes into strict training. They do it to get a crown that will not last; but we do it to get a crown that will last forever. Therefore I do not run like a man running aimlessly; I do not fight like a man beating the air. No, I beat my body and make it my slave so that after I have preached to others, I myself will not be disqualified for the prize."

### For further study

Acts 24:25; 1 Corinthians 6:12-20; 1 Corinthians 7:7-9; Galatians 5:19-26; 2 Timothy 3:1-5; Titus 1:7-8; 2 Peter 1:5-7

# The fruit of gentleness: Humble love

**Gentleness is the opposite of self-righteous stubbornness. Gentle people can easily submit to God and to others.**

I f gentleness is a weakness in your life, other people sometimes perceive you as self-righteous. A big step toward becoming a more loving person might be to pay less attention to your own rights.

### Understanding the term

The Greek term for gentleness, *praytes,* means the opposite of argumentative, self-righteous stubbornness. Gentle people don't find it difficult to submit to God and to others. They don't easily react in an angry way. Instead, they tend to be mild, tolerant, and humbly disposed toward others.

Gentleness, as a matter of principle, refrains from using any kind of force against sinners. According to 1 Timothy 3:3, leaders in particular should be characterized by gentleness.

Jesus gave a model for the kind of gentleness that he expects of us when he washed his disciples' feet, as recorded in John 13. At the end of this passage, Jesus said, "Now that I, your Lord and Teacher, have washed your feet, you also should wash one another's feet. I have set you an example that you should do as I have done for you" (John 13:14-15).

### Color segment

Since gentleness is a spiritually motivated mildness, as opposed to the "tougher" aspects of love that we can find in the red segment, we have placed it at the center of the blue segment (grace).

### Key Bible passage: Galatians 6:1-3

"If someone is caught in a sin, you who are spiritual should restore him gently. But watch yourself, or you also may be tempted. Carry each other's burden, and in this way you will fulfill the law of Christ. If anyone thinks he is something when he is nothing, he deceives himself."

### For further study

Matthew 5:5; Matthew 11:28-30; John 8:3-11; Ephesians 4:1-3; 2 Timothy 2:24-26; Titus 3:1-2; James 1:19-21; 1 Peter 3:15-17

# Love is indivisible

We have seen that love, as described in the Bible and modeled by Jesus Christ himself, covers an extremely wide spectrum. If you take another look at the eight terms in our spiritual color wheel on page 59, it's apparent at first sight that the biblical concept of love literally touches all dimensions of your life: your spirituality and your family, your job and your neighborhood, your political views and your social involvement, your church activities and your view of different theological traditions, your earthly activities and your life after death.

For this reason some people find this teaching threatening. They try to put love in chains. They don't actually deny the Christian concept of love, but restrict it to certain areas of life, preferring to ignore the others. This reaction is so widespread that I would presume all of us are tempted to fall into this trap to one degree or another.

### Ovations and boos

Years ago, at a big conference in Germany, I experienced a dramatic example of how these mechanisms work. At that conference, it was my task to do a public interview with the German television journalist Franz Alt, who was at that time one of the most popular and controversial faces on German TV. His book on peace and justice had just been published and had immediately become the number one best-selling political book in post-war Germany. The thesis of his book, a plea for non-violence and disarmament, made Franz Alt a hero of the European peace and civil rights movement.

> Love is by definition holistic, indivisible. It affects the microcosm as well as the macrocosm.

During our interview, he explained his radical views and received loud ovations from the 6,000-person audience—almost exclusively members or advocates of the peace movement. Once he had the people completely on his side, Franz shouted into the applauding audience, "This commitment to life is also a commitment to unborn life! There is no peace in Germany as long as abortion is taken for granted and no longer recognized as a problem..."

The applause stopped abruptly. Loud boos filled the hall. Some women tried to force their way onto the platform, demanding I give them the same speaking right as Franz to propagate their views. It was a militant, aggressive atmosphere.

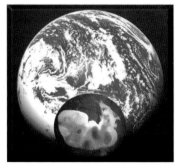

### A modern schizophrenia

After the meeting came to an end, I asked Franz why he had been so provocative. He must have known what reaction to expect from this kind of audience. He smiled. "Of course I knew. But I think that this is a typical example of our modern schizophrenia—people always pick out the issues that suit them and don't see that the message of Jesus must be taken as a whole. As long as disarmament is a hobby-horse of the left and abortion a hobby-horse of the right, we haven't understood anything. Both sides are concerned about life—but unfortunately only about parts of life. That is what makes the struggle of both sides so hopeless and boring."

### Not just the private sphere

Again and again we have to deal with this kind of schizophrenia. We try to limit, split, and divide love. One of the most widespread methods, especially in Christianity, is to limit love to the private sphere. The Greeks had a special expression to describe those unpolitical people who believed that true love could only be expressed in the private realm. They called those people *idiotes.* Originally, "idiot" was just another word for "private citizen." It seems that there are far too many *idiotes,* even among Christians!

People who claim to love their family, but who are unloving at work, only show a partial love. I doubt whether this sort of love is actually love at all, because love by definition is holistic, indivisible. It affects the microcosm as well as the macrocosm. Erich Fromm rightly said, "Love is not first of all a relationship to a particular person. It is an attitude, a character-orientation that determines the relationship of a person to the world as a whole, and not just to a single object of love."

Even if love has its origin in heaven, it must always come down to earth.

### The breath of the soul

Some people think that it is proof of the intensity of their love to love no one and nothing other than the one single object of their affection. But that is wrong. Love is like breathing. If someone were to tell you, "I only breathe when I'm with you," you would probably not believe that person—and rightly so. Why? He would be dead if he didn't breathe when he was apart from you. Love is the breath of the soul. It is not true that you only have a certain amount of "love energy" available and have to budget it. Either you make an effort to be a loving person—and your love will gradually color all areas of your life—or you just don't understand what love is all about.

### Coming down to earth

It's one thing to demand these things on platforms and in books, and it's a completely different thing to put them into practice. That is the exclusive task of the remaining pages of this book: practical exercises targeted at helping you infuse "three-colored love" into the trivial realities of life.

Even if love has its origin in heaven, it must always come down to earth. Therefore, in the final two chapters we will focus on how to apply the principles studied so far both to your personal life (chapter 3) and to the life of your church (chapter 4).

# Twelve exercises that can revolutionize your life

*There are plenty of reformers prepared to reform other people. Only a few are prepared to reform themselves. But nothing is more revolutionary than a quiet reformation of ourselves. This chapter offers practical suggestions for starting such a process. Each of the exercises concentrates on one of the three different aspects of love—justice, truth, or grace.*

**Chapter 3:
Personal growth**

# Exercise 1:
# Fill up with God's love

You can only pass on what you have previously received. If you don't know anything, you can only pass on ignorance. If you have no joy, you can only pass on despair. If you have no inner freedom, you can only lock others out. You can only give away what you have. Therefore you should do all you can to be filled to the brim with the best thing there is on this earth—the love of God.

It would be counterproductive to try to produce love in our own strength. That would simply lead to new bondage that would further distance us from the love of God. Many Christians experience very little of God's love because they try—with great seriousness and admirable commitment—to live according to God's will in their own strength. However, love is not equivalent to performing a lot of loving actions. It requires, first of all, that we be fully immersed into God's love ourselves.

> People experience God's love in a great variety of ways. In many cases, it is connected to a moment of surprise.

### The source of love

The Bible says, "God has poured out his love into our hearts by the Holy Spirit, who he has given us" (Rom. 5:5). In other words, if you are a Christian, you don't have to produce love; you merely have to open yourself up to the love of God so that it can flow through you to other people. God's love is the source and the stream. Your contribution is simply to keep the "channel" intact.

Have you ever seen the impressive aqueducts that were once used to supply the entire city of Rome with fresh water? Even though they still give us an impression of their former function, today they are a pitiful sight. The bold arches are broken down, and the supporting pillars are no more than rubble. No matter how much water gushes from the spring, the water cannot reach the city because the channel is not intact. The better connected you are to the source, the more love will flow through you to other people.

### Theory and practice

Most Christians understand this theory very well. The problem is that, although they accept it with their minds, they have not truly *experienced* that God loves them. What is the use of being told to open yourself up to the love of God if no one tells you how to do it?

It is certainly true that a believer has God's love whether he or she feels it or not. But it is also true that God's love can only show its real *power* in one's life when it is experienced, when it literally "flows through" every part of one's being.

### How people experience the love of God

How can that happen in practice? It is important to answer this question, however, any answer we give has its risks. People experience

God's love in a great variety of ways. In many cases, it is connected to a moment of surprise. At any rate, there is no specific method that applies to everyone.

As I have conversed with Christians, I have collected many different answers to the question of how they have experienced God's love in practice. Here are some of their answers:

> **You don't have to produce love; your task is merely to open yourself for the love of God so that it can flow through you to other people.**

- "In a very intimate conversation with my personal counselor."

- "In quiet prayer at home, when suddenly the whole room was so filled with the love of God that I could actually feel it physically."

- "After my wife had left me, when a Christian brother from my church came and put his arm around me."

- "When a sermon spoke to me so personally that I cried with happiness for hours afterwards."

- "When I was healed from a serious illness."

- "In my last vacation by the sea, when I could relax."

- "When Christians laid their hands on me and prayed for the Holy Spirit to fill me from top to bottom."

- "In the last worship service, during the Lord's supper."

- "Whenever I consciously take time for Bible study and meditation."

These are wonderful testimonies of Christians who have encountered the love of God in different ways. The problem is that most people think that what has been helpful in their own experience must also be helpful for everyone else. But that is not true.

### God deals differently with different people

Someone who found a single hearty hug to be a real breakthrough in his life could tend to see hugging as *the* answer to experiencing God's love. If he is not careful, he might soon get on a lot of people's nerves. If a person had a deep experience of God's love following the laying on of hands and prayer, she may think that this is *the* way in which everyone experiences God's love. But that doesn't work either. God reveals his love to people in diverse ways.

As you start working through the following instructions, please regard them merely as suggestions. Many Christians have experienced the love of God in a new way as a result of these exercises. In my seminars we have had encouraging experiences with them. It may well be that God will use some of these ideas to show you more of his love. But do not think of them as "the answer," but just as what they are—suggestions.

# Your turn:

In the restless routine of our lives we often forget how much God loves us. Just reminding ourselves of this fact can work wonders.

- ***I am loved:*** *The time between waking and sleeping is important for the following exercise. During that period of time we are conscious, but still have easy access to our subconscious. Our subconscious is not selective and does not criticize, but it is receptive to everything that it perceives. It records all of our impressions, almost like a tape-recorder. Therefore, we must be careful that what we tell ourselves really conforms to the truth of God.*

*Tell yourself every evening before falling asleep (or every morning immediately after waking up): "I am loved by God." Repeat this statement 20 times. The constant repetition helps to mold your subconscious with this truth. In your head, you already know it. Now, through this exercise, you will be allowing that knowledge to move from your head to your whole being, including your emotions.*

- ***Give thanks every morning:*** *Thank God every morning for his love. You don't need to create love—it's already there! An attitude of constant thankfulness will help you let God's love influence your feelings more and more.*

- ***Eyes for God's daily provisions:*** *It can be misleading to expect manifestations of God's love exclusively in the area of the extraordinary. Most of us are surrounded by an abundance of God's gracious daily provisions: a pair of shoes, running water, a place to sleep, etc. The next time you encounter one of these expressions of God's love (such as putting on your shoes, turning on the water-tap, going to bed, etc.) close your eyes for a few seconds. Remind yourself that God has chosen to provide you with all of this because he loves you so much. Thank him for these expressions of his love to you.*

- ***Loving stumbling stones:*** *Fix pieces of paper on which you have written, "You are loved!", in all sorts of places where you will "stumble over" them. Or set your watch to bleep every hour. Each time it bleeps, or each time you stumble over a note, pause for five seconds, take a deep breath, and say to yourself, "Now I'll breathe out all restlessness and breathe in God's love." You will notice that this simple exercise can have a very beneficial effect. In the restless routine of our lives we often forget how much God loves us. Just reminding ourselves of this fact can work wonders.*

# Exercise 2:
# Love yourself

A frightening number of Christians believe that it is a virtue to love others, but a sure sign of egotism to love oneself. However, there are three good reasons for including love of ourselves in our efforts to grow in love:

- The Bible speaks of loving ourselves. "Love your neighbor as yourself," Jesus said (Matt. 19:19). Love for ourselves is taken so seriously in the Bible that it is used as the standard by which we should measure our love for others.

- Love is indivisible (see page 79). Erich Fromm was right when he wrote, "If it is a virtue to love my neighbor as a human being, it must also be a virtue—and not a vice—to love myself, because I am also a human being." Love is an attitude which stays the same for all objects of love—including yourself.

- You are only able to love others if you love yourself. You can only give away what you are. If you find yourself unattractive, you can only give others something unattractive—and who really wants to do that? Augustine said, "If you can't love yourself, you can't truly love your neighbor."

**You are only able to love others if you love yourself. If you find yourself unattractive, you can only give others something unattractive—and who really wants to do that?**

### Self-love: the opposite of self-centeredness

In some groups, the idea of self-love is met with resistance. It is thought to be a sign of self-centeredness, egotism, and self-infatuation. But, in reality, self-love is exactly the opposite of self-centeredness. Self-centered people do not really love themselves. Actually, they suffer from the fact that they have never found peace with themselves, that they have never learned to accept themselves, along with their faults and weaknesses, as a creation of God. That is why they are so dependent on receiving affirmation from others. Their ego needs to be satisfied. They are not in a position to give love to others.

Only people who have learned to accept themselves can let themselves go and be "self-less." People who have not yet "discovered" themselves are constantly searching for themselves and become, literally, self-seeking and egocentric. Walter Trobisch, who wrote a wonderful little book called *Love Yourself,* put it succinctly: "Anyone who does not love himself is an egoist."

People with a strong self-identity can afford to put an end to their ego-trip. In contrast to people with a weak self-identity who are inwardly dependent on the admiration of others, they no longer need to make themselves the center of all things.

### Self-love has to be learned

Nobody is born with this kind of self-love. We have to learn it, just like we have to learn to love others. People who don't learn to love themselves, will have difficulties with most of the exercises in this book. They are liable to become people who "love" exclusively out of obligation—an attitude that not only becomes martyrdom for themselves, but also for others.

I have met many Christians who proudly point out how "selfless" they are, but whose broken sense of self-identify could clearly be sensed. It is a tragedy that such an attitude is even encouraged in some churches. Often these people cannot understand why their relationships with other people are unsatisfying, especially when they are always so "available." Sometimes they even believe that their unhappiness is the price of genuine love and selflessness. In reality, it is the price for their failure to learn the art of making friends with themselves.

**People with a strong self-identity can afford to stop their ego-trip. They no longer need to make themselves the center of all things.**

## Your turn:

• ***Enjoy your reflection:*** *When did you last have a good look at your own face in a mirror? Not just when washing, shaving or putting on make-up, but taking time to "read" your own face? Try it. Take exactly five minutes for this exercise. Then write down what you felt as you did so. Our experiments with this exercise have shown that these five minutes reveal a surprising amount of information about how far we can love and accept ourselves.*

• ***What you like about yourself:*** *Write down everything you like about yourself. Then read this list out loud, thank God for it—and enjoy it!*

• ***Being alone:*** *People who don't love themselves often find it difficult to be alone. It is good for every one of us to make a point of learning to be alone—without reading, listening to the radio, watching TV, calling friends on the mobile phone, using the computer, or eating. Take a full hour for this exercise. Afterwards, write down what you felt.*

# Exercise 3: Wear other people's glasses

While the first two exercises focused on how you as a Christian can experience love, the following exercises concentrate on some practical steps you can take in order to pass on to others the love you have received.

Perhaps the most important principle of love is to see the world through other people's eyes. Why do they act the way they do? What influences have caused them to be the way they are? What are their fears, their dreams, their longings? Ask these questions over and over again, particularly with people you find difficult to relate to.

> Perhaps the most important principle of love is to see the world through other people's eyes.

### "Love your enemies"

Jesus told us that just loving those who love us is not enough (Matt. 5:46-47). His demands are clear: "Love your enemies and pray for those who persecute you, that you may be sons of your Father in heaven. He causes his sun to rise on the evil and the good, and sends rain on the righteous and the unrighteous" (Matt. 5:44-45). We have already seen that loving our enemies is at the very core of a genuine Christian understanding of love (page 47).

I have learned much about the power of this principle from Pastor Heinrich Albertz, the former Mayor of Berlin who became famous worldwide after a prominent German politician was kidnapped by terrorists. In exchange for the politician, the kidnappers demanded the release of many terrorists from prison, and asked Heinrich Albertz to be a voluntary hostage to accompany the freed terrorists on their flight to Aden. There he found himself, on a plane, shoulder to shoulder with the elite of German terrorists, whose actions had earned the wrath of the honest citizens of the nation, in an extremely volatile situation in which the lives of all were in jeopardy.

Some time after these dramatic events, I visited Heinrich Albertz. I wanted to know whether he had felt like throttling those terrorists in the 30 or 40 critical hours they spent together. "Not in the least," he answered. "The whole project was only possible because a certain amount of mutual trust was present from the outset. If anyone had been aggressive, things would have come to a dreadful end." And he added, "On a purely human level, our interaction was not like that anyway. The young people I was dealing with treated me as I would have wished my own children to treat me."

### Why mere disgust is no help

With passion in his voice, Heinrich Albertz emphasized that he had treated the terrorists as human beings, "no more and no less." He said, "Very few humans are criminals, and all criminals are humans." I asked him whether it might not be a sign of moral health to feel disgust toward acts of terrorist violence and those who commit them.

Albertz shrugged his shoulders. "What good does disgust do? Disgust achieves nothing. It doesn't help us out of the vicious circle of violence. It has troubled me for years that our society has not been prepared to ask what influence it has had in causing these young people to turn to violence. I have never been so simplistic as to suggest that everything is society's fault. I have always said that every individual who murders or kidnaps bears an untransferable personal responsibility. But our society has not been willing to hear the message that these things happen within a context. Those of us who pointed this out from the beginning, and pointed it out clearly, were branded as sympathizers, or even semi-terrorists, ourselves."

> We tend to erect a taboo barrier between our ego and our anti-ego, a sort of psychological Berlin Wall, which protects us from recognizing that evil is our own shadow.

I found these words hard to hear—until I realized that they hit the nail straight on the head. It seems to me that Christians, in particular, love to prove their own morality by passionately expressing their disgust at all forms of immorality. "Disgusting inhuman terrorists!" "What kind of mother would murder her own child in the womb!" "Freaking nuclear genocidist!" "What type of lunatic monster would choose to be a neo-Nazi skinhead?!" "Unbelievable, how those commie pigs tyrannize their country." "What a scandal sexual immorality is among young people today!" We say these things and feel that we are morally superior to all of these people. We are the goodies, and they are the baddies. Our disgust at their evil deeds is all the proof we need.

### Recognizing the "terrorist in yourself"

We will only learn to love when we recognize ourselves in the other person: in the terrorist, the abortionist, the atomic bomber, the skinhead, the communist, or the adulterer. If our own morality only expresses itself in disgust at immorality, we are in danger of dividing people into two categories, the good and the bad. We, of course, are on the good side, inwardly and outwardly separated from the other side. We erect a taboo barrier between our ego and our anti-ego, a sort of psychological Berlin Wall, which protects us from recognizing that evil is our own shadow.

Admit your own anger, and the murderer will no longer seem like an incomprehensible monster. Recognize the slave and the master within yourself, and you will feel more for masochists and sadists. Recognize your own paralysis in the face of economic greed and military self-righteousness, and you will no longer see terrorists as wild animals. Admit your own death wish, and you will be able to show empathy with people who want to commit suicide. Recognize your own fear of taking risks, of swimming against the tide, and you will notice that the potential informant is also in you.

### The danger of labels

People who are not prepared to recognize part of themselves (possibly a very much repressed part) in others will spend all of their time building walls to keep the rabble away. They label others and consider the matter closed. He is a Jew. A Black. A Muslim. A political activist. A hippie. A capitalist. A tree-hugger. An incurable conservative. A punk. – End of story!

What is a punk anyway. Is he able to love? Can he radiate grace? How does he relate to his friends? Does he have children? Can he weep? Is he happy? Is there something he can give to others? These are the important considerations—not the fact that he is a punk, a black, a Jew, a liberal, or a reactionary.

The ability to see the world from another person's point of view doesn't come easily to us. We have to practice it. If we don't practice this art, we will soon see the police as "pigs," demonstrators as "stone throwers," socialists as "atheists," Muslims as "fundamentalists," church planters as "sectarians," charismatics as "demonized," non-charismatics as "unspiritual," Protestants as "heretics," Catholics as "the whore of Babylon." Believe me, meeting thousands of Christians every year in all sorts of contexts, I have collected more of these labels than there are countries in the world. The sad thing is that most people don't even realize that these are expressions of highly ideological thinking—right in the midst of the Christian church.

> Wouldn't it be great if our churches could celebrate parties because Christians had managed to demolish the walls previously built up in their own heads and hearts?

### How walls come down

This is how walls between people come into being. They divide every bit as much as the Berlin Wall divided the city. Of course, anyone who builds such walls will spend a great amount of energy justifying their actions. The Department of Propaganda in their own minds works overtime. A real ideologist will not only sell his wall to others as an anti-fascist (or anti-sectarian, anti-pluralistic, anti-terrorist, anti-atheistic) protective wall— he will actually buy it himself. Poor ideologist!

Friends, let's have a wall-demolishing party! That's the best thing to do with these walls. When I heard on the car radio in 1989 that the Berlin Wall was open, I drove straight to Berlin and was one of those who hammered a hole in that demonic wall. Every stone we knocked out was a reason to lift the champagne-filled Dixie Cups to celebrate with friends from East and West. It was a gigantic party, a wonderful celebration. The only people who couldn't celebrate were those for whom not only the wall was collapsing, but also the ideology they had built their lives upon.

Wouldn't it be great if our churches could party like that because Christians had managed to demolish the walls previously built up in their own heads and hearts? I'd be glad to pay for the champagne (and the Dixie Cups)!

> The ability to see the world from another person's point of view doesn't come easily to us. We have to train it.

## Your turn:

• **Living with yourself:** *Ask yourself the following question: If I had to live with someone who was exactly like me, what would I want to change in that person? Write your answers down. This can be a good first step toward seeing yourself through the eyes of those around you.*

• **I am you:** *In this exercise, put yourself in the place of someone whose convictions you find hard to accept. For instance: a conservative could put himself in the place of a liberal, a charismatic in the place of an anti-charismatic, a pacifist in the place of a soldier, a pro-life activist in the place of a woman who has had an abortion, etc.*

*Do this at a time when you have a certain degree of control over your feelings. Find a quiet place to be alone. Relax and close your eyes. Recall a particular past encounter with this person. Allow it to pass before your "inner eyes," remembering it in all its detail. Resist any temptation to try to understand the other person. Rather, summon together all the imagination you are capable of and place yourself in the other person's shoes. Relive the same situation; try to visualize the same people and hear the same conversation as if it were the original encounter, but this time completely from the other person's point of view. Try to feel the impact of each word spoken just as the other person might have felt it. Try to understand what they meant for him or her.*

*You will discover that this exercise helps you see the world through another person's eyes. When you have finished, write an account of your feelings throughout the different stages of the exercise. As I have experimented with this in my seminars, I have discovered that the first three or four times people try this exercise they find it difficult, but that it gets easier with each effort.*

• **Empathic conversation:** *Make an effort to get into a real conversion with someone whose convictions you are unable to come to terms with. Throughout the conversation, only ask questions that will enable that person to make his or her position clearer. Don't argue. Try to put yourself—including your feelings—in the other person's shoes for the duration of the conversation. Prepare the way for this dialogue by asking God to give you great sensitivity and understanding. Following the conversation, write down your thoughts and discoveries.*

# Exercise 4: Put an end to spiritual hypocrisy

Chapter 3: Personal growth

Although it is important to see the world through the eyes of another person, this principle must never lead us to hypocrisy. There are Christians who are repeatedly dishonest and justify their behavior by saying that they do it to protect others' feelings.

But love has nothing in common with hypocrisy. The Danish philosopher Søren Kierkegaard said, "The best weapon against hypocrisy is love; it is not just a weapon, but a gaping chasm, and in all eternity it has nothing in common with hypocrisy."

### The liturgy of hypocrisy

However, there are churches in which institutionalized hypocrisy appears to have become part of their liturgy. People are so accustomed to it that they no longer recognize that they are telling downright lies.

"The sermon was riveting," we say when actually we almost fell asleep. We gush with excitement, "What a lovely dress!", while wondering how on earth anyone could be so fashion-challenged. We declare with wet eyes how deeply moved we were by a special number, when in reality we were cringing with pain because the guitarist had not tuned his guitar. We effusively say thank you for presents that we later store away in the basement; we admire homes that we think are abominably decorated; we compliment someone who has just won a gold medal in incompetence. If we continue in this vein, our declarations won't be worth the paper they're printed on—and rightly so.

> There are churches in which institutionalized hypocrisy appears to have become part of their liturgy.

If we confront people about these untruths, they will usually say, "It's true that I was a little less than honest. But I didn't want to hurt the person's feelings." It sounds like they have taken seriously the principle of seeing things through another person's eyes (exercise 3). But actually, the very opposite is true. Most of these lies are purely *self*-protection. We want to save *ourselves* trouble and unpleasantness. We manipulate the truth to make life more comfortable for *ourselves* (see page 32).

### Dishonesty can be very unloving

It is true that the truth sometimes hurts, but it can be a hundred times more painful to be constantly lied to by someone we love. Such lies, however "well-meaning" they may be, can destroy trust forever.

We must be able to rely on the fact that those who love us will be honest with us and tell us the truth. They are the only ones who would dare to tell me after lunch that I still have a piece of spaghetti in my beard. Anyone else would let me spend the rest of the day with the spaghetti dangling off my face. A loving person will say, "By the way, you have a spaghetti noodle in your beard."

### Friendly ways of telling the truth

Who says that we can only tell people the truth in a way that hurts? There are also friendly ways to do it. We don't have to say, "Your sermon bored my socks off." We can say, "I didn't find this sermon nearly as lively and meaningful as the one last week. But that's just my opinion, and I'm not Billy Graham."

Or imagine that someone comes to visit you at the worst possible time and says, "I hope I'm not disturbing you." You don't need to say, "No, not at all, actually I was waiting for you all day long!", nor do you have to say, "Leave my house immediately, you hunchback!" You could say, for example, "Actually, right now is not a good time for me. But I'd love to talk to you on the phone this evening. Would six o'clock be all right?" That is honest—and loving. As we have seen in the first chapter, truth and love are no contradiction. Rather, truth is an integral part of genuine love.

### Expectations in different cultures

I am well aware that different cultures have different and even contradicting mechanisms, traditions, and expectations in this area. There are cultures that are, to use our terminology, traditionally strong in the area of truth (red) and relatively weak in the area of grace (blue). There are others where it is just the other way around: They are relatively strong in "blue," and weaker in "red" (see pages 44-45). It goes without saying that for some cultures the exercises covered in this section will be more difficult than for others. In some situations, it may go against cultural expectations to behave in the ways suggested here. Does this mean that the exercises provided are not applicable in these cultures, as I have at times been told?

> Who says that we can only tell people the truth in a way that hurts? There are also friendly ways to do it.

On the contrary. If the cultural expectations should be in conflict with some of the love principles we deal with in this book, we need to invest *even more* energy into those areas. We should never confuse a popular societal behavior pattern with behavior that might be most helpful or most needed.

The wonderful thing is that, throughout the course of this book, each culture will identify principles in which it is traditionally strong, and others that could be considered "collective deficits." There will be some exercises that are especially difficult for Asian cultures, others will be particularly difficult for Westerners, and others, for people in countries of the Southern hemisphere. In other words, all of us have strengths, and all of us have growth edges. This realization does not seem to be a bad starting point for a cultural exchange in an age of globalization.

### Different exercises for different muscles

Never forget that the main focus of these exercises is not to practice love, but to "train our love muscles" (see page 51). The different exercises in this book are intended to train different love muscles. Thus the motto of one exercise is "Wear other people's glasses," while the next one teaches you to "Be yourself." The more exercises you do, the better you will be prepared to react lovingly in new and unique situations.

> The different exercises in this book are intended to train different "love muscles."

# Your turn:

• **Shocking honesty:** *This exercise is not for people of an anxious disposition. Decide that for one week you will take literally absolutely everything other people say to you. If someone says, "I'll pray for you" (but really wanted to communicate "I will think about you"), give him or her a whole list of prayer requests and later ask how he or she is doing with your prayer list. If the waiter in a restaurant asks how you liked the food, and the food was really dreadful, say, "It was absolutely dreadful, sir." When people ask, "How are you doing?", give them a detailed account of the way you feel at that moment. And enjoy their puzzlement!*

*Please note: I am not saying that the suggested reactions are the best way to deal with others. Don't forget that this is just an exercise to teach you and other people how much human communication—even among Christians—is made up of thoughtless and sometimes even dishonest comments. The goal of this exercise is to reveal just that.*

*Of course, normally your dealings with others should be more tactful. However, having once done this exercise, you will have a better sense of when certain comments are just a polite way of treating each other—and when they are plain lies. You will probably also discover that in many cases it is not love, but simply the fear of an uncomfortable situation that hinders us from speaking the truth.*

• **Situations in which you were not honest:** *Each evening for a week, write down every situation that arose throughout the day in which you were not completely honest. Then ask yourself the following questions about each situation:*

1. *Did I act like that because it was the most loving way to relate to the other person in this specific situation?*

2. *Did I act like that because I was a coward (too intent on avoiding conflict or too keen on preserving harmony) and therefore unable to tell the truth?*

# Exercise 5:
# Learn to trust

Have you heard the story about the man who was driving up a winding, narrow mountain road? As he came around a particularly narrow bend, a woman approaching from the opposite direction, stuck her head out of the car window and shouted, "Pig!" The man shouted back, "You swine!" Upon rounding the bend, he ran over a pig.

**Only those who dare to trust are able to give love to others.**

My intention here is not to focus primarily on the poor pig (that was killed) nor on the poor woman (who was insulted), but rather on the poor man (whose distrust was the core root of the events that followed). Many of us find it difficult to believe that others are prepared to treat us well. When we actually encounter people who do, a well-trained inner reflex is activated that suspects them of ulterior motives.

### Presents? No thanks!

I personally enjoy giving small gifts to people I don't know, just to make them happy. Sometimes I take presents to my seminars to give to the participants. When I do this, people usually think that it must have something to do with what I plan to teach, and wait for an "explanation." However, there is no explanation. I do it for the pure fun of it.

On occasion, when I was living in Hamburg, Germany, I would go to the shopping center and hand out coins (of the approximate value of a dollar each) to passers-by. The various reactions I received were a far more eloquent study on "trust" than any psychological text-book could offer.

One lady immediately quickened her pace when I offered her the coin, almost as if I had made an indecent proposal.

Another lady grabbed her son's hand, which was eagerly reaching out for the coin, pulled him away, slapped the surprised boy on the hand, and said with a frown, "You mustn't do such things!"

An elderly man made an insulting gesture and yelled in a hysterical voice, "You anarchist pig!"

Others asked me why I was doing it, and I answered truthfully, "To brighten your day." For many, that brought an end to their sympathetic posture. "Somebody like you should be in a nut house," one person shouted in contempt.

Some people grabbed the coin and rushed away like frightened pigeons, as if they had captured something.

Do you know what? Less than 10 percent accepted the coin, thanked me, and seemed to be happy. In other words, less than 10 percent behaved like normal people who have no reason to suspect someone's motives. If you don't believe me, try it for yourself. Don't worry about becoming poor. Provided that you don't do it in a slum area, most people will walk right past you and simply ignore the gift that you offer them.

### The trust questionnaire

Many people are reluctant to trust others because they fear that if they are too trusting, they will be taken advantage of. But is this a justified fear? Or could it be that this widespread expectation is a sheer myth?

Dr. Julian Rotter of the University of Connecticut has done long-term research to test the effects of trust on personality development. He used an extensive questionnaire to determine whether each person showed a high, medium, or low level of trust. Then he tested the people in each category to determine their intelligence quotients and other characteristics. The answers to the following questions are based on this study. Before you look at the correct answers, check whether you believe the following statements are true or false.

| True | False | |
|------|-------|---|
| ❑ | ❑ | 1. People with a high level of trust tend to be more gullible than others. |
| ❑ | ❑ | 2. People with a high level of trust have a lower intelligence quotient than people who are less trusting. |
| ❑ | ❑ | 3. People with a high level of trust are happier than people who are less trusting. |
| ❑ | ❑ | 4. People with a high level of trust are more trustworthy than others. |
| ❑ | ❑ | 5. People with a high level of trust are more liable to be taken in by tricksters. |

> Many people are reluctant to trust others because they fear that if they are too trusting, they will be taken advantage of.

According to the studies conducted by Dr. Rotter, the answers are as follows: 1. false, 2. false, 3. true, 4. true, 5. false. That means that people with a high level of trust aren't more gullible, less intelligent, and easier to trick than more skeptical people. Moreover, they are happier. Only those who dare to trust are able to give love to others.

### The center of our faith

What I have called "trust" in this section is called "faith" in most Bible translations. We have seen before that the terms "truth," "trust," "faith," and "faithfulness" are treated as synonyms in many passages of Scripture (see pages 20-22, 32-33, 74). People who want to feel secure by never venturing outside their comfort zones ought to ask some radical questions about their own faith. Trust is at the opposite pole of seeking security, yet at the same time it provides the only soil on which true security can grow.

Even if we try to present the practical exercises in this chapter as simply as possible in order not to overload them with theological reflections, we should always keep in mind that we are not dealing with fun and games, but with the basic questions of our Christian faith.

To solve the most crucial world issues such as prejudice, racial conflict, and war, the world urgently needs people who are deeply rooted in trust. Millions of dollars invested in an effort to solve these problems won't achieve anything if they are in the hands of people who don't trust each other. However, millions of people who have learned how to trust, wouldn't need a dime to be able to achieve the goals of these programs.

Where are these people? I hope that you are one of them. And if you do not consider yourself a member of this army yet, I hope you will join the training program that will help recruit trusting soldiers of love. Our world needs them badly.

# Your turn:

**Trust is at the opposite pole of seeking security, yet at the same time it provides the only soil on which true security can grow.**

• **Situations in which you trust:** *If you find it difficult to trust people, this exercise will help you. Make a list of as many real life situations as possible in which you trust people without difficulty (e.g. bus drivers, doctors, postal workers, airline pilots). Then make a second list of as many situations as possible in which you find it difficult to trust people.*

*Now reflect on the situations in which you easily trust others, and imagine what your behavior would be if you had no trust (e.g. "How can I know that the bus driver is not going to cause an accident?"). Think about what you would do if you lost all trust in these situations and how people around you would react. Record your thoughts on paper.*

*Now turn things around. Think of situations in which you normally find it difficult to trust and imagine how your behavior and the reactions of those around you would change if you did trust. Once again, record your thoughts. How does this exercise effect your attitude toward life.*

• **Let yourself fall:** *If you are part of a small group, conduct the following experiment. Have one of the participants stand in the middle of the room with his or her eyes closed. Have six others stand behind this person in two rows of three facing each other. Have these six individuals firmly join their hands or arms and ask the first volunteer to fall backwards. When the team of six catches this person, have them carry him or her around the room. Give everyone in the group a turn to fall and be carried. Afterwards, discuss your reactions.*

# Exercise 6: Make yourself vulnerable

**M**any of us have developed protective shells around ourselves that we don't even notice. Behind them, there is a secret oath, "Never again am I going to experience the pain of being rejected like that."

All of us have our wounds and hurts from trying to become more loving people. Many people have designed a heavy suit of armor around their soul to protect them from further injury. But we should never forget that we pay a high price for the protection provided by such armor. In the Middle Ages, if a knight in armor fell from his horse, he could hardly make it to his feet unless someone helped him. Our emotional armor can make us just as stiff and immobile—especially if it effectively protects us from emotional hurt.

> The emotional armor not only keeps our enemies at a distance, but also our friends.

Our emotional armor not only keeps our enemies at a distance, but also our friends. The greatest danger, however, is that this emotional armor can prevent us from experiencing the love of God. Just as this armor prevents love from flowing from us to others, it also prevents love from flowing to us from others.

### No risk, no reward

Love requires the courage to take off our armor and make ourselves vulnerable. That is a risk. But we cannot have love at a lower price. This is the point in the process where we are faced with a decision. In several of my seminars, I have noticed that it is precisely at this point that people become fearful, because they don't want to make themselves vulnerable once again to the pain they have previously experienced.

I understand this fear very well. When we invest love and receive indifference or even rejection, it is disappointing and often hurtful. The pain of rejected love is one of the strongest imaginable forms of emotional pain. Loving a plant is far less complicated because it involves less risk. The plant cannot hurt you like a person can.

### Three practical suggestions

And yet, we can't expect to grow in love without making ourselves vulnerable. If you find it difficult to make yourself vulnerable, the following thoughts may be of help.

*1. We should free ourselves from the utopian idea that everyone ought to like us.*

Imagine you are the most beautiful, delicious fruit in the world—perhaps a ripe, juicy apple—offering your delectable taste to those around you. You must remember that, even if you are the most tasty apple in the world, there are people who just don't like apples. There will always be someone whom you love, but who doesn't like you, the best tasting apple in the world, because this person prefers bananas. You could, of course, decide to become a banana. But you must realize that, at best, you can only be a second-class banana. It's only as an apple that you can be the best in the world. You could spend your whole life trying to be the best banana in the world, but it won't happen because you are an apple. Or you could content yourself with being the best apple and simply accept the fact that there are some people who don't like apples.

> You can lay a table with the choicest food, but you can never force someone to eat. Love gives everyone the freedom to accept or to say no.

*2. We should always anticipate that some invitations will be rejected.*

You can lay a table with the choicest food, but you can never force someone to eat. Love gives everyone the freedom to accept or to say no. Everyone who issues an invitation should recognize that it is normal for an offer to be rejected. When that happens, we must not take it as a personal affront. People who only accept our invitations for fear of hurting our feelings are not doing us a favor.

*3. We will only be invulnerable when we are dead.*

Life means being vulnerable. Mental health includes the willingness to accept hurt. The only place that guarantees the absence of hurt is death. If we want to find out what it means to live, and not just to vegetate, we must be willing to give up our "security" mentality. C.S. Lewis expressed this well: "Love something—and your heart is sure to suffer torment, and perhaps to break. If you want to be sure of protecting it, you should give your heart to no one, not even to an animal."

### The precondition for happiness

Without a doubt, a loving person is more vulnerable than someone who doesn't dare to love. But do not get the impression that being vulnerable is bound to cause unhappiness. The opposite is true. The willingness to be vulnerable is a precondition for being a truly happy person.

This is the only way you can experience the ecstasy (even if only for a few precious moments) of seeing your feelings of alienation replaced by a sense of belonging. You discover that you are not alone. You notice the mysterious vibrations that link your soul with the soul of another person. You feel vulnerable, but at the same time protected. Your body relaxes. The blood flows more easily through your arteries and veins. Your breathing becomes freer. Your emotional armor softens. The defense mechanisms you have developed in order to cope with a hostile world disappear. The giving of yourself opens a door out of your inner self. You experience yourself as you really are.

Have you ever sensed these feelings pulsing through you? If so, you will not likely wish to crawl back into your emotional armor.

# Your turn:

• **Fear of being vulnerable:** *Look at the following table. On the left side is a list of thoughts that reveal a fear of vulnerability in a given situation. On the right is a list of responses that can help eliminate or reduce each fear. Develop a similar table with your own examples.*

| **Fear of vulnerability** | **Helpful thoughts** |
|---|---|
| *If I show my feelings, I risk being thought sentimental.* | *Is it really more attractive to be non-sentimental?* |
| *If I reveal my dreams in public, I risk being thought crazy.* | *Actually, most people are envious of those who are free to be somewhat crazy.* |
| *If I issue an invitation, my offer may be rejected.* | *If this happens, I will have my own personal party on that very evening—just for myself.* |

**Living means being vulnerable. The only place that guarantees we will not receive any more hurt is death.**

• **Negative experiences:** *Write down situations in which you have made yourself vulnerable and have then been hurt. These negative experiences can be an enormous hindrance to your efforts to grow in love. Bring these situations to God in prayer. Ask him to help you avoid building up walls that prevent you from making yourself vulnerable in the future. It might be good to discuss these hurts with an experienced counselor.*

• **Rejected invitations:** *Within the coming week, extend an invitation (to a meal, a worship service at church, a Christian meeting, etc.) to one or several people that you expect will reject your offer. Examine your feelings when this happens. Can you take it in stride? The more often you do this, the more relaxed you will become.*

# Exercise 7:
# Dare to forgive

I learned an impressive lesson about the liberating power of forgiveness when I met Pastor Uwe Holmer from Berlin. In the revolutionary events of 1989, Erich Honecker—the man responsible for building the Berlin Wall in 1961—was deposed as the Communist head of state in East Germany. After he was discharged from the hospital, he was literally homeless. It was the Holmer family who took the ex-dictator and his wife into their home and offered them hospitality. At the very time when the hatred of the people against *the* personification of the oppressive regime was at its climax, the Holmers set an example of forgiveness.

> While countless people were longing to get their hands on the deposed dictator, the Holmer family set an example of forgiveness.

Pastor Holmer was greatly criticized for his action. He stressed again and again that his family didn't take this step out of sympathy for the old political system. They, too, had been negatively effected by the communist regime. In East Germany, children of families with church affiliations were often refused admission to the upper grades of high school, making it impossible for them to qualify for college education. The Holmers have ten children, and eight of them applied for admission to that level of high school. In spite of excellent grades, none of them was accepted. Pastor Holmer said, "Yet we hold no bitterness in our hearts, because we are followers of our Lord and have forgiven."

### How anger disappeared

One week after Erich Honecker and his wife had left the pastor's house (the Soviet President Michael Gorbachev had taken care of him), I visited the Holmers. I wanted to observe for myself whether or not they really held no grudge against this man who was chiefly responsible for the system that had caused their family—and the whole country—so much suffering.

Uwe Holmer told me that he had certainly held grudges in the past, but when the Honeckers stood before him at the entrance of his house, he found that his grudge had vanished. "I was surprised at myself," Uwe Holmer told me, "my past anger toward the government was suddenly gone. But you know, for years it has been the forgiveness of my Lord that has sustained me. I know that my Lord wants me to forgive others. When you've lived under forgiveness for a long time, it's not so terribly hard to forgive others."

### Understanding the dictator

I asked him if now, having lived with Erich Honecker for two months, he could better understand why this man had become the person he was. "Yes, I can understand him a bit better now," he said. "I see him as a communist who came from a working class family that had been through very hard times. For him, Christianity was identical to exploitation—at least, that's how he saw it as a child—so becoming a Communist was a logical step in his development. Later he was arrested by the Nazis and spent ten years in prison. Finally, he was freed by the Red Army. From his perspective, it was his comrades who had freed him."

### And the victims?

While the Honeckers were staying with the Holmer family, the pastor's house was almost constantly surrounded by angry citizens who were waiting—some of them with great anger—to get their hands on the deposed dictator. I asked Uwe Holmer whether he could understand these people, too.

"Yes, I can understand them very well," he said. "I especially remember one man who said to me, 'I spent 15 years in prison, I was condemned to death.' His wife stood next to him and said, 'You cannot imagine what I've been through under this regime. You should not forgive so easily.' I then explained to them, 'What you say really strikes a chord in my heart. You have suffered much more than I have, and I have not forgiven Honecker in your place. But still I ask you: Do you have any alternative to forgiving Mr. Honecker? If you don't, the poison of bitterness and anger will remain in your heart and will never leave you in peace.' The man then admitted, 'You're right, there is no other way. I want to forgive, too.' Jesus said, 'If you do not forgive men their sins, your Father will not forgive you.' In the first place, my forgiveness for Mr. Honecker has nothing to do with Mr. Honecker, but with me."

I have quoted extensively from my conversation with Uwe Holmer, because he has really understood how we need to live if Christian love is not to remain a hollow idea. Even the Communist Egon Krenz, who succeeded Honecker as the head of state until he, too, had to resign under the pressure of the masses, was impressed by Pastor Holmer's action. He admitted, "Once again, it is the church that teaches us a tolerance that we as Communists were not capable of."

### Evil isn't harmless

The actions of Uwe Holmer did not meet only with approval. A prominent American church leader told me, "I just don't understand it. All Honecker deserved was to be executed." This taught me an important distinction that is often overlooked. It is the distinction between two very different ways of responding to evil. One way is fitting for a Christian, the other isn't. The distinction lies between forgiveness and pretending that evil is harmless by excusing everything, accepting what is absolutely unacceptable, and being indifferent toward evil. There is very little, if anything at all, that Christians can excuse in this way—but they can *forgive* anything of those they choose to love.

> You forgive those who have wronged you by learning to forgive.

### A learning process

You forgive those who have done you wrong by *learning* to forgive. Even Uwe Holmer had to learn this through a long, painful process. If you don't face up to this learning process, you will constantly carry accumulated anger and hurt on your shoulders, which will weigh on you like a heavy burden pressing you to the ground. But when you learn to forgive, you are released from this burden, and your newly released energy can be used to grow more in love.

For me, it was a moving moment when, after the fall of the Berlin Wall, thousands of German believers used the earlier version of this book to start a twelve-week campaign that our institute had initiated, and followed the motto, "Take stones from the wall to build bridges." Richard von Weizsäcker, the German President at the time, wrote me saying, "Now that the treaties have been signed, the re-unification of Germans must take place in their hearts and heads. Your campaign will contribute to this." Interestingly enough, even Erich Honecker—the man who built the Berlin Wall—wrote that the love shared "will bring strength and courage back" to the people.

# Your turn:

When you've lived under forgiveness for a long time, it's not so terribly hard to forgive others.

• **Prayer of forgiveness:** *Think of a person who has done you wrong. What is your attitude toward that person today? What problems are not yet resolved? What could have been done differently—and how? Bring these situations to the Lord in prayer and declare that you forgive this person.*

• **Re-living painful situations:** *If you think you cannot forgive, try the following: Go to a place where you can be undisturbed for at least one hour. Re-live your feelings of pain. Don't just think about your hurt feelings—feel them again, even if it is painful. If you sense the urge to weep, don't hold back your tears. Remind yourself that Jesus is close to you in this situation. Feel his closeness, his love, and his willingness to forgive. Remember that you are completely dependent on the fact that he has forgiven you. Speak to the person you cannot forgive and say: "I forgive you."*

• **A gift of forgiveness:** *If people do you wrong during the coming week, determine to do two things: First, forgive them immediately. The best way to do this is in prayer. Second, give a small gift to the person you have forgiven. It is best if the gift is in some way related to your conflict. Observe the effect this has on your own feelings.*

• **Asking for forgiveness:** *When you catch yourself in the act of doing wrong to someone else, say to this person at once, "I'm so sorry. Please forgive me." Observe the effect this has on the other person.*

# Exercise 8:
# Be transparent

People who want to grow in love must make an effort to be transparent in every area of their lives. The more transparent you are, the less your life will be like an inaccessible fortress. It will be more like one of those Dutch homes that has no curtains so that you can look in from the street and see right through to the back yard (and, of course, everything in between). There is nothing hidden, and there is nothing that people feel a need to hide.

This sort of transparency requires courage. Thus, many people try to grow in love (in the terms of the above metaphor) by decorating the front garden of their house with pretty flowers, rather than opening up the house itself. They are afraid that others might discover things about them that would make them appear in an unfavorable light. Yet transparency is the most valuable contribution we can make to a loving relationship, because it's the only way we can truly give ourselves to others.

> Many people try to grow in love by decorating the front garden of their house with pretty flowers, rather than opening up the house itself.

### Practical hints

Here are some hints about what we can do to make our relationships with others more transparent.

*1. Avoid empty chatter.*

By "empty chatter" I mean words that just fill space, which could be filled just as easily, and perhaps better, with bubble wrap. It is pure filling material. Silence is much better than empty chatter. Who says you have to talk all the time?

Empty chatter is anything we say that is not motivated by love. It doesn't really matter whether it is primitive beer-house talk, jokes intended to demonstrate your superiority, unloving talk about other people, or high-sounding theological discourse simply meant to show how well-read or educated or sophisticated you are. Having had numerous opportunities to teach at universities, I can tell you that the most educated people are sometimes the most unbearable windbags.

*2. Learn not to hide your feelings.*

Some communication seminars teach the exact opposite of this point: How to act in such a way that others cannot tell what you are feeling. How to give the impression of self-confidence when you are full of misgivings. How to appear happy when you actually feel like crying.

Each one of us is capable of strong emotion, and it is highly unnatural to hide it. But it can be learned, and most of us have become quite good at it. However, love teaches us to reveal our feelings. When you lack confidence, it is alright for others around you to notice. Why hide it by pretending to be full of confidence? If you feel like bursting into laughter, why not do so? A good laugh will not only do you good, it may well be a release for others, too. If you feel like crying, don't try to suppress it. Let your tears flow. Hiding our feelings is a convention that requires a great deal of effort, but is of no benefit whatsoever to you or to the people around you.

*3. Express your expectations of others.*

Loving people are not mind readers. Therefore, express your expectations. Just as you demonstrate your love for others, you should communicate to them your need to be loved. Don't expect others, however close to you they may be, to know your needs and feelings if you haven't articulated them.

In one seminar, I asked the participants to put into words their expectations of others. The exercise started quite slowly, but then those who voiced their wishes were surprised at the wonderful reactions they got from others in the group. One person said, "I'd never have imagined that you felt lonely. You always seem to connect with people so quickly." Someone else said, "I'm glad to know that you want us to pray for you. You always give the impression of being so strong and self-assured, as if you could do everything in your own strength." A number of other needs were revealed that could probably never have been met if they had not been explicitly voiced.

> Some Christians are plagued by a fear of physical contact, and would benefit greatly if they were freed from this fear.

*4. Don't be afraid of physical contact.*

Some Christians are plagued by a fear of physical contact, and would benefit greatly if they were freed from this fear. A simple handshake or an arm around the shoulder can sometimes do far more than the most thoughtful words.

I heard that Mother Teresa did not allow her missionaries to wear gloves when washing people who were dying and worm-ridden. In spite of the potential hazard of infection, there was good reason to strictly observe this policy. Plastic gloves would non-verbally communicate the very opposite of what Mother Teresa strove to communicate in her ministry. In a world full of the danger of infection, we learn to keep our distance. It might cost a little to let others actually feel our presence, but it is one of the simplest, most loving statements we can make.

*5. Share in the joy of others—and let them share in your joy.*

Loving includes sharing our joy with others. If you see something beautiful, point it out to someone. If you see a beautiful person, tell him or her, "You are very beautiful!" And then it's probably wise to make a quick escape and give this person a chance to recover from the shock.

Sharing in the joys of others is, I think, a surer sign of real love than giving sympathy in suffering; though that, done in the right way, is also an important part of loving. It is fairly common for someone who is going through a trial to find others to support him or her. But I have frequently noticed that when a Christian is successful, fellow Christians do not share in this joy, but see it as a cause of deep unhappiness and envy.

I have collected many examples of this phenomenon. For example, if a pastor has a quickly growing church, do the pastors of the neighboring churches rejoice with him? Far from it—in many cases he is met by deep suspicion and ill-founded accusation.

Or what happens when a Christian experiences a spectacular answer to prayer? Can he be sure that his fellow Christians will rejoice with him? Not necessarily. Often the response is something like this: "Who does he think he is, a saint or something?"

**Each one of us is capable of strong emotion, and it is highly unnatural to hide it.**

In many cases, envy and jealousy have taken the place of spontaneous, sincere joy. As a result, many people are terribly alone in their experience of joy—and that can be as frustrating as being alone in times of sadness.

The early church was so radiant that even skeptics were attracted by it—"See how they love each other!" That was their secret: They were not a perfect community, but they were a fellowship in which people were prepared to share in each other's joys and sorrows.

### Enjoy it!

Do you know what happens when you let another person into your life? Suddenly you have four eyes, not two. You have two heads and four arms. You have two opportunities to experience joy and happiness, and two opportunities to be sad and to weep. In other words, your life becomes fuller. Sharing moves you from "I" to "we."

These experiences are some of the deepest we have. We get into conversations that last late into the night. For a few happy moments, time seems to stand still. We reveal our deepest feelings. Our words flow. One act of trust leads to another. Enjoy these experiences. Love is a party that should not only be prepared, but also celebrated.

# Your turn:

Love is a party that should not only be prepared, but also celebrated.

• *I appreciate you:* For the next week, when you are with people you love and appreciate, tell them so. Try to say it very honestly and in a unique way for each person. Observe your-self—the words you say, the way you use non-verbal communication such as touch, giving gifts, etc. Write down your experiences.

• *Positive and negative attitudes:* For this exercise, find a partner who will play by the same rules. Face your partner, close your eyes and concentrate for one minute on some positive aspect of the other person. Then open your eyes and look at your partner. Take note of how it feels to have a positive attitude toward the other person. Change roles.

Version 2: When you close your eyes, concentrate on either a positive or a negative aspect of the other person. When you open your eyes, the other person must guess whether you were thinking positive or negative thoughts. You will be surprised at how clearly the other person notices your inner attitude, even if you don't say a word.

• *Voice your expectations:* Write down things that others could do to make your life more pleasant, but that you have never before mentioned to them. By voicing these, you will make it easier for them to love you. In the course of the coming week, speak to several people about these things. And don't be taken aback if they are surprised at your wishes.

# Exercise 9: Train active listening

**M**ark Twain once wanted to prove that nobody listened to anybody at a New York party because everybody was just talking for the sake of talking. He arrived late at a party. The hostess received him and said, "Come in darling. Here is the Malaysian ambassador. Let me introduce you ..."

"Please excuse my lack of punctuality," said Mark Twain, "I had to strangle my old aunt, and it took rather longer than I expected."

The hostess replied, "I'm so glad you could come nevertheless."

## Listening must be learned

Even in Christian groups, many conversations are marked by an astonishing, almost ritualistic superficiality that is every bit as dramatic as the incident reported by Mark Twain. Real listening is an art we need to practice. It is much more than just hearing words. When we truly listen to others, we communicate, "I'm listening to you because I respect you. I'm interested in you."

I am not particularly gifted in the art of active listening, so I am all the more grateful for the few occasions when I have helped people by just listening to them. I remember a young pastor who came up to me after a seminar and asked, "Could I have a word with you about my church?" He told me with great emotion about a rather difficult situation. His associate pastor was continually opposing him, the church leadership was made up of traditionalists, his health had been poor for some time, and he felt his theological training had not really prepared him for church development. He confessed his fear of returning to his church when the seminar was over. The whole time he was speaking, I looked into his eyes, genuinely felt sympathy, and did not say a word.

> We have two ears and only one tongue so that we can listen more and speak less.

After he had spoken for about ten minutes, he drew a deep breath and sighed with relief. He put his arms around me and said, "Christian, you've helped me so much." Actually, I hadn't said a single word. It was not that I had planned to practice the art of active listening. Rather, his predicament had left me speechless. I just did not know what to say. But listening in that short encounter obviously helped that pastor more than all the well thought-out words I had said throughout the seminar.

## Two ears—and only one tongue!

We all know how difficult it is to talk with self-centered people who don't listen, but seem to spend all of their time thinking about their next profound response. They use what the other person says as a springboard for sharing their favorite ideas. Perhaps Diogenes was thinking of people like that when he said more than two thousand years ago, "We have two ears and only one tongue so that we can hear more and speak less." The Apostle James expressed it like this, "My dear brothers, take note of this: Everyone should be quick to listen, slow to speak and slow to become angry" (James 1:19). Active listening is an art, and the reason it is so difficult is that the human brain can assimilate information much faster than a person can talk. It is estimated that we can process 400 to 600 words per minute, while the average person can only talk at a rate of 200 to 300 words per minute.

### Roots and fruit

However, none of us should believe that active listening is a mere technical issue: Incorporate the proper gestures (such as nodding your head), learn to ask the right questions ("Did I understand correctly, that you..."), practice good eye contact—and *voilà*, we have produced another active listener! Due to the great need for active listening, there are a lot of training courses that have a primarily (if not exclusively) technical approach. I don't doubt that even such techniques are of some value; but they should not be confused with the art of active listening as an expression of genuine love. They clearly focus on secondary virtues, overlooking the dimension of primary virtues completely (see pages 41-43).

> Growth in love is the root; active listening is a natural fruit. We should never try to reverse this sequence.

The best training doesn't start with skills. Since the ability to listen is dependent on genuine interest in the other person, it has a lot to do with your own character. You have to be sincerely interested in other people, and not just pretend to be interested. People who are rooted in the three colors of love—justice, truth, and (especially) grace—will be good listeners as a natural result. Growth in love is the root; active listening is a natural fruit. We should never try to reverse this sequence.

### Practical tips

Once this has been understood, it makes sense to deal with some technical aspects of listening as well. As long as we don't regard them as substitutes for becoming more loving people, these skills can be quite helpful:

- Concentrate consciously on the other person. At first you may fear that this will exhaust you, but the opposite is true. Any activity we do with our full concentration actually keeps us awake, whereas activities we perform without concentration make us sleepy.

- Take note of your partners' body language, tone of speech, and what is communicated "between the lines."

- Don't jump to conclusions about what the other person is trying to communicate. If you think you know beforehand what somebody wants to say, that is usually what you will hear—whether this person actually says it or not.

- Ask questions to make sure you have really understood. Many people are reluctant to ask questions because they want to avoid giving the impression that they weren't listening properly the first time.
- Look the other person in the eye. Eye contact is one of the best ways of forcing ourselves to listen actively.
- Make appropriate comments to show that you have understood what the other person is saying. Repeat his or her thoughts in your own words.

Active listening communicates, "I understand what you are feeling." This is neither agreeing nor disagreeing. You are not judging whether their feelings are right or wrong. It is a form of affirming another person, and it is usually greatly appreciated as it is an attitude seldom encountered. That may explain why active listening is such a powerful way of expressing love.

Stand back to back while talking to each other. This is the communication practiced by Christians who are defending their points of view, without taking interest in the other person.

# Your turn:

- **Remembering details:** *Throughout the coming day, decide to listen very carefully whenever someone tells you something that would normally not be of interest to you. Remember the details. Write them down. A few days later, ask the other person about them and observe what effect this has both on you and on others. Repeat this exercise frequently.*

- **Back to back:** *For the following exercise you will need a partner. Stand back to back and start talking to each other. This is a physical representation of the kind of communication practiced by Christians who are more interested in defending their own point of view than understanding the other person. Do some self-examination. Are there some subjects for which you find this kind of communication more difficult than for others?*

- **Feedback:** *Choose a partner who is also aware of the "rules" and has a conflicting opinion on a controversial topic. Carry on a conversation together about that topic. The rules are as follows. When person A has expressed an opinion, person B must repeat it until A signals that he or she feels that B has understood. Only then can B express his or her opinion, but this time A has to prove that he was understood. The first time I did this exercise, I found that I was a complete failure in this area of communication (especially when discussing a subject that emotionally riles me). It was only after I had practiced it several times that my ability to give a fair summary of the other person's view improved.*

# Exercise 10:
# Surprise with gifts

**A**n old adage says that "love is not love until you give it away." As long as it does not express itself in a tangible act, love is no more than a nice idea—a sheer proposition, an empty word, an abstract concept. One of the best ways of expressing our love for other people is to surprise them with a gift. Thomas Aquinas said, "Love is the original gift. Everything else which may be given to us unearned only becomes a gift through love." A gift, in its essence, is something undeserved. Your salary, for instance, is not a gift. You have earned it, you have (usually) worked hard for it. A gift, however, is something altogether different. You get it simply because someone loves you. It's an expression of grace.

### Giving others joy for Jesus's sake

One of the people who has made gift-giving a way of life is pastor Paul Deitenbeck, one of the most prominent spokesmen of the German evangelical movement. I have visited him at his home twice. The first time, he gave me an extra-large bar of chocolate; the second time, a five-mark coin. "But don't go putting it in the offering," he added. Friends of the Deitenbeck family tell me that all of their visitors are treated that way. It's simply not possible to come out of the Deitenbeck household without receiving at least one small gift.

*A real present should always be a surprise.*

When Paul Deitenbeck goes to the butcher during the Christmas season, it is not a surprise to hear him say, "I'm so glad that Christ was born. Butcher, please give everyone in the shop a piece of sausage and put it on my bill." He says of himself, "When they bury me, I want it to be said of me that I was eager to give people joy for Jesus' sake. I'm not particularly trying to convert them. I just want to make them happy."

I learned from Paul Deitenbeck that real giving has nothing to do with the conventional gift-giving rituals that most of us know so well. There are gifts that make life richer and more colorful, and others that only heighten monotony and routine. A friend of mine who works as a TV journalist told me that he once had to cover a major church anniversary celebration. All sorts of people—clothed in black suits and boring gray ties—had come to offer their congratulations to the bishop and offer him their gifts.

This friend told me that there was not a single present that would be in any way useful for the bishop or his wife. Just about every person gave him a copper engraving of an old church or some similar motif, and garnished this act with a flourish of verbiage that interested no one. How boring! The poor bishop routinely showed his admiration for each and every engraving ("What an interesting motif!"), but it was obvious that not one of the presents came as a surprise to him. I had to wonder what the poor bishop would do with all these copper engravings. They would probably collect dust along with the multitudinous engravings from previous anniversaries in the basement of the diocesan offices.

### Endless possibilities

A real present should be a surprise. Take flowers to someone who never gets flowers. Ask someone's opinion on a subject he knows a lot about, then just let him talk. Give your bishop a yellow carnation and a piece of real licorice (but please, not another copper engraving). Invite someone to the theater. Call a lonely, elderly person on the phone and invite him or her out on a trip to the grocery store. Let someone talk to you for two hours—and never say the word "I."

> There are gifts that make life more colorful, and others which only heighten monotony and routine.

If we surprise people with gifts, we shouldn't expect to receive something in return. Such expectations are the root cause of conventional gift-giving rituals. I am aware that there are cultures where it is against good manners not to give something in return. This is the secondary virtue of "politeness," and in that context it is certainly important to stick to this cultural convention. But even there, don't forget to focus on the primary virtue—the undeserved, the surprise.

In one of my seminars on love, I asked the participants to give each other a gift. They had just half an hour, and the shops in the neighborhood were already closed. At first, people were not sure what this exercise was meant to achieve. But the result was overwhelming. One woman was given a Bible verse which had a "prophetic" impact on her life. Another person had his car washed for him. A hymn sung in several parts was given to a third. It was wonderful. At the end, everyone spoke warmly of the love they had experienced in this group. The pastor told me that six months later the church was still talking about this exercise. Why not enrich each other's lives in this way more often? I'm sure God likes the idea.

# Your turn:

• **The 5 dollar gift:** *Within the next 48 hours, give someone a gift that costs no more than $5. You will notice that if you make an effort to give a relatively simple gift, the effect will often be greater than if you choose a standard flower arrangement for $20 or a boring box of chocolates for $10.*

*By the way, if you don't know who would be happy to receive such a present, feel free to send one to me. Here is my address: Christian A. Schwarz, c/o NCD International, Diedersbueller Str. 6, 25924 Emmelsbuell, Germany. You can be absolutely sure that in me you will find a recipient who will sincerely enjoy every single present I receive (as long as it is not a copper engraving).*

**Chapter 3:
Personal growth**

# Exercise 11:
# Use your humor

For many non-Christians, the church is the last place on earth where they would expect to find joy and humor. What is worse, the same is true of many Christians. A lot of churches have achieved a frightening degree of perfection in their lack of joy and humor. Everything is serious and somber, and if ever loud, spontaneous laughter should be heard, everyone assumes there must be a drunk in their midst. Christians don't do such things.

*The ability to laugh at ourselves and our own shortcomings is an act of faith, a proof of our trust in the God who loves us as we are.*

### Lack of humor and lack of love

There is a clearly identifiable link between a lack of humor and a lack of love. For instance, in many churches where love is lacking, laughter is as well. In our research, we have compared the love quotient with the humor quotient of Christian churches. The correlation is striking.

It is my experience that faith without humor can quickly turn into dogmatism and legalism, self-righteousness and fanaticism. People who take themselves with deadly seriousness, wind up creating an environment that smells of death. Ideologists cannot laugh at themselves, because that laughter would be the end of their ideology.

It is this "no laughter" mentality, combined with the "Michael Kohlhaas neurosis" of self-righteousness that causes so many of our churches to be groups of people with no radiance, no attractiveness.

### Humor breaks down tension

There is hardly anything that opens the door for getting close to strangers more than laughter. We have all experienced times when a good laugh has transformed a tense, fearful relationship into a warm, cheerful, productive one.

I am often invited to speak on fairly emotional and controversial subjects. Sometimes within the same audience there are people that are in violent conflict with one another due to their highly opposing views. I can very clearly sense when the opposing parties are just waiting to see whether my arguments will support their position or the "enemy" position. When that is the case, I am usually confronted with a lot of grim faces. There is terrific tension in the air, and I am driven to pray, "Lord, how can your Spirit influence our conference in an atmosphere like this?"

I have noticed on a number of occasions the liberating effect of using humor, whether it be by showing a cartoon that portrays the positions of the two opposing groups from an unusual and very human perspective, by telling a story that pokes fun at our own shortcomings, or by telling a joke that expresses my own nervousness about dealing with such an awkward situation.

The reaction has always been the same. The participants have leaned back, relaxed, and crossed their legs. The tension has disappeared from their faces. Their voices have sounded less fanatical. All of a sudden, I have found myself looking into friendly eyes and have noticed that people were listening with greater interest. The discussion has become deeper, more loving, more spiritual. And all of this simply happened because people had a chance to laugh about things that up to then had only been talked of in defensive, angry ways: "I'm right. You're wrong."

Cheerfulness, humor, and laughter are wonderful and easy-to-use tools for breaking down relational barriers between people. They enable us to reduce inhibitions and tension. They create a positive atmosphere and are—as confirmed by medical research—an effective remedy for depression. "If I didn't have a sense of humor," Mahatma Gandhi is reported to say, "I would have committed suicide long ago."

**Laugh at yourself!**

Of course there are malicious, dirty, humiliating, and hurtful kinds of humor. I am certainly not recommending that kind of pseudo-humor. I mean the sort of humor that enables you to laugh at *yourself*—especially at your weaknesses.

I have been in a number of situations in which the only thing that has saved me was my ability to see the funny side of the situation and to laugh at myself and my imperfections. Since I made the decision to always be the first to laugh at my weaknesses, I have enjoyed far greater emotional stability. Therefore, if other people also laugh at me, I am prepared to join in their laughter. This has enabled me to deal with criticism far more easily.

> For many non-Christians, the church is the last place on earth where they would expect to find joy and humor. What is worse, the same applies for many Christians.

If you cannot laugh at yourself, you will find it difficult to accept yourself as you are. And if you cannot come to terms with who you are, it will be difficult for you to accept others as they are. That is why people without a sense of humor are often unable to love.

Humor reminds us that we aren't perfect. Dictators and fanatics—including Christian fanatics—rarely have a sense of humor because they think of themselves as perfect. When things get funny, they are not at all amused.

Humor helps us forget our self-righteous high and mightiness. It is a demonstration that we can rise above the pitiful state of the narrow-minded thinking that we sometimes find ourselves in. The ability to laugh at ourselves and our own shortcomings is an act of faith, a proof of our trust in the God who loves us as we are.

In our research, we have compared the love quotient with the humor quotient of Christian churches. The correlation is striking.

## Your turn:

• **How humor can break up tension:** Try to recall at least one situation you have experienced in which humor helped to relax the atmosphere in a tense situation. Write this situation down.

• **Smiling forbidden:** To get a better feeling for the important and positive role of laughing and smiling, determine not to laugh or smile for a whole day. Evaluate your experience at the end of that day.

*Most people who have done this exercise have reported that they had to stop the exercise after a few hours—some even after a few minutes—because they had the feeling, "I just cannot live like that." That is the whole point of this exercise. How long can you keep it up?*

• **Laughing at yourself:** Next time something you do goes wrong, don't criticize yourself, but have a good laugh at your shortcomings instead. Tell others about your mistake so that they can laugh with you. You may have to train in this area quite a bit before you will experience the results. However, you can be sure that laughing at yourself is something that you can learn—and it actually makes you a happier person.

# Exercise 12: Have a meal together

I spent one of the most beautiful days of my life in the small Italian coastal town of Camogli. The town has a one-of-a-kind festival known as *Sagra del Pesce*. Everyone in the harbor is invited to eat fish from the pan. On that day, the friendly hosts tip a hundredweight of fish at a time into what is probably the largest pan in the world. It is a matter of honor that both the inhabitants of Camogli and their guests eat for free.

Just imagine the scene. Hundreds of people who don't even know each other gathered around an enormous pan, church bells ringing, flags blowing, the penetrating smell of fish in every corner, hands sticky with grease, Italian wine being poured out, people singing, dancing, and raising their glasses together—until late into the night. You may have doubts about the quality of the fish, but you have no doubt about the friendliness of the people of Camogli. There you are, a total stranger, invited to eat as much as you'd like. Mamma mia, what hosts!

Most people who know me are aware that eating is one of my great passions. I love the smell and taste of well-prepared food. Even more than the food, I love the fellowship of people with whom I can sit around a table for hours, solving all of the world's problems. My favorite foods are Moussaka, Sushi, Raclette, Churasco al radiccio, Gado-Gado, Aguacates con gambas, Dim Sim, Gorgonzola lamb Ana María style, Kimch'i, kangaroo on minced lentils, stuffed peppers, mango chutney, Korean dog meat, Ginseng tee, banana ice cream ... and just about everything that I have been served by loving people.

### Shared meals and church growth

When we did our research on the reasons for church growth, among hundreds of other interesting discoveries, one truth came to light for which I was particularly glad. In growing churches, Christians invite each other for meals or coffee an average of 16 times per year. In declining churches that number is reduced to 10. There is a correlation between inviting people for meals and the growth of the church. Isn't that delicious?

**Shared meals or tea times are wonderful ways of experiencing how love can be expressed in practical terms.**

Cynics have suggested that the growth of larger churches is not related to the number of attendees, but to their total weight. But that is not true. It is statistically demonstrable that churches in which people frequently invite each other for meals or coffee are more likely to grow than others. I am not surprised by this. Shared meals or tea times are wonderful ways of experiencing how love can be expressed in practical terms. And loving churches, as the same survey showed, are usually growing churches.

It's a good sign when church meetings begin with a shared meal. Don't be afraid that nothing "productive" will take place during this time. On the contrary—every shared meal in a friendly atmosphere increases the "love quotient" of the group. And a group with a high love quotient can expect to be attractive to others and grow. What more could you want?

### Shared meals in the Bible

> There is a correlation between inviting people for meals and the growth of the church. Isn't that delicious?

It is no accident that the Bible speaks of shared meals at so many decisive points. This begins in the earliest books of the Scriptures, when God's covenant with his people is celebrated with a shared meal (Ex. 24:11). And it continues right up to the final pages of Revelation, where we read, "Blessed are those who are invited to the wedding supper of the Lamb" (Rev. 19:9). In between, we are told in many places of the sacramental significance of shared meals. Jesus called the tax collector Zacchaeus down from a tree to eat with him, he fed 5,000 people with bread and fish, he made sure that the wine at a wedding would not run out—in the Bible, we come across shared meals again and again.

Do you want to make a significant contribution to church growth? Then do the following: Invite somebody over for a meal. If you can't cook, no problem. Just put a frozen pizza in the oven. Or fetch a couple of BigMacs from the nearest McDonald's. Then place a vase with flowers on the table, insert Schubert's "Trout Quintet" into your CD player, light a candle, thank God for his presence—and enjoy the experience!

## Your turn:

- ***An invitation:*** *Over the course of the coming week, reach out to someone by inviting him or her to a meal (either in a restaurant or in your home). During this time, try to apply several of the principles that you have learned from this book. Observe the effect this has on your guest. Afterwards, go through the following list and check how many principles you applied:*

|  | Applied | Not applied |
|---|---|---|
| Wear other people's glasses (exercise 3) | ❑ | ❑ |
| Put an end to spiritual hypocrisy (exercise 4) | ❑ | ❑ |
| Learn to trust (exercise 5) | ❑ | ❑ |
| Make yourself vulnerable (exercise 6) | ❑ | ❑ |
| Dare to forgive (exercise 7) | ❑ | ❑ |
| Be transparent (exercise 8) | ❑ | ❑ |
| Train active listening (exercise 9) | ❑ | ❑ |
| Surprise with gifts (exercise 10) | ❑ | ❑ |
| Use your humor (exercise 11) | ❑ | ❑ |

# Eight exercises to transform your church into an oasis of love

*It can be quite powerful when people see the light of God's love shine through an individual believer. However, God has ordained an even more powerful force: a group of believers, or even a whole church, that reflects the different colors of his love. This chapter is all about bringing this divine concept down to earth. Groups that apply the following eight principles will begin to notice that people are almost magnetically attracted to them.*

**Chapter 4:
Growing together**

# Exercise 1: "Give off your scent, gentlemen!"

T wo Western missionaries once visited the Hindu Mahatma Gandhi. They wanted to learn what they needed to do in order to help Indians better understand Jesus. "Ponder the secret of the rose," Gandhi said. "It doesn't do anything, it just smells. That's why everybody loves it. Therefore, give off your scent, gentlemen!" We are told that the missionaries went away perplexed. They had evidently expected to be given a strategy for leading Indians to faith in Jesus Christ. The advice, "Give off your scent" obviously didn't seem to fit into their evangelistic tool box.

> Ponder the secret of the rose. It doesn't do anything, it just smells. That's why everybody loves it.

When I heard this story, it dawned on me at once that the "aroma principle" that Gandhi described is a key to church growth. The Bible uses similar language: "We are to God the aroma of Christ among those who are being saved and those who are perishing" (2 Cor. 2:15). Christian churches ought to be places where the sweet scent of Jesus draws people in for a closer look.

### The aroma of life

People don't want to hear our theories about love. They want to experience love. And I think they have a right to expect that. Jesus himself described how the "aroma principle" works in practical terms: "All men will know that you are my disciples if you love one another" (John 13:35). Love gives off a fragrance. In the midst of a world full of the stench of death, Christians ought to spread the aroma of life. How can this climate be nurtured in a group or church?

Think again about the "three color paradigm" that we have dealt with in the first two chapters of this book. When you look at worldwide Christianity, the problem is not that one specific color is missing altogether. On the contrary! There are many groups involved in social justice (green segment), committed to establishing the standards of God's kingdom in the political arena—and distancing themselves from Christians who have a different agenda. There are many other groups truly committed to biblical truth (red segment), focused on the Word of God—and fighting against Christians who reflect green or blue. Finally, we find many groups that stress God's grace (blue segment), focused on acceptance and tolerance—and condemning those who are not like them.

The problem is not in the colors each of these groups reflect; it is not even in the colors they don't reflect. The problem is that they distance themselves from groups that reflect colors other than their own. They are often right when they criticize others of being one-sided, and of leaving out essential parts of the Christian message. But they fail to see how one-sided they are themselves. And they fail to see that they often invest their best energy fighting against others, rather than giving off the wonderful scent of God's love. To spread this aroma, we need to create a healthy, joyful, inviting atmosphere in our Christian circles.

Unfortunately, many Christian groups are marked by an atmosphere of self-righteousness, dogmatism, and resistance to all that is new. They display an "anti-everything" attitude, which opposes everyone and everything that is beyond their own horizon. Those groups, however significant their contributions in a specific color segment might be, cannot expect to give off the wonderful aroma of God's love.

### Meeting other traditions

If we want to grow in love, we must stop thinking only in terms of the narrow categories presented in our own churches. Meeting with Christians from different traditions (whether from another country, another denomination, another theological background, or another philosophy of ministry) often leads to wonderful learning experiences. Helmut Gollwitzer, a pastor and university professor, who was one of the handful that resisted Hitler, along with individuals like Dietrich Bonhoeffer, has taught me a lot about this. Later in his life, he got involved with many diverse groups in church and society, which made him one of the most controversial public figures in post-war Germany. He had strong relationships to the "establishment" as well as to the "outcasts" of society; he performed the funeral not only for the German president but also for the most prominent terrorist, who had committed suicide in prison. You can probably imagine what many people thought of him!

Liberal groups called him an "evangelical" (meant as an insult), evangelicals called him a "political activist" (also meant as an insult), terrorists called him a "reactionary," and the spokesman of the conservative party called him "the father of terrorism." Helmut Gollwitzer was not disturbed by these labels. Why not? He told me that the gospel had set him free from being afraid of relating to people of any sort. He once wrote the following in a letter to me, words that I chose to make the motto of my life: "You cannot lock up the gospel—neither in orthodox prisons, nor in liberal, evangelical, Barthian prisons, with their frequent prior judgements of what the gospel may say and what it may not say, what spheres of life it may affect and what it may not. It moves in its own power, and where it moves, it transcends our differences and leads people together."

**People don't want to hear our theories about love. They want to experience love.**

## A group experiment:

• *Invite a Christian from a different, perhaps conflicting, church tradition to visit your group. Ask this person to talk about his or her experience with God. As you interact with this person, try to apply the principles you have learned in this book. As a group, agree beforehand that you won't argue with this person, rather, you will listen and try to learn about the different ways God works in and through different groups.*

**Chapter 4:**
**Growing together**

# Exercise 2:
# "Just for the fun of it"

B ack in the 1970's my father developed a church growth program that became known far beyond the boundaries of our area. It was basically a visitation program aimed at helping people who did not yet know Christ find a personal relationship with him.

### The spring greeting

The program included one activity which we particularly enjoyed. It was called the "spring greeting" and worked like this: At the beginning of spring, all of the church members who were interested in taking part in the program would meet half an hour before the regularly scheduled meeting. Prior to their arrival, numerous bouquets of daffodils would have been prepared, and each person was given two of them to deliver to two households in the neighborhood. There were just two rules they had to follow:

- *Rule 1:* They had to present the flowers and say, "It's spring. We're from the church and would like to give you these flowers. We hope you enjoy them."

- *Rule 2:* If the church members were asked why they were doing it (and you can be sure that they were always asked), they were not allowed to say anything about the blood of the Lamb or the joy of salvation (or give any other spiritual explanation). Instead, they were supposed to say, "*Just for the fun of it. We are happy, and we would like you to be happy, too.*"

> "It's spring. We are happy, and we would like you to be happy, too."

Wherever this program was put into practice according to these two rules, the reactions were overwhelmingly positive. Those visited were overjoyed beyond belief, and the church members were thankful that they didn't have to hand out church propaganda or collect money, but could simply do something that would bring joy to everyone involved *just for the fun of it.*

### "Scripture reading and prayer"

As I mentioned, other churches heard of this program, and the "spring greeting" was carried out in many places. I well remember one evening when it was planned for a church that was located in a part of Germany called Siegerland. For those who are not familiar with the spiritual geography of Germany, this is one of the most "pious" areas of the whole country. It is said that people in the Siegerland region can get converted as many as three times in just one worship service!

It was the first time that this exercise had been carried out in a rural area. The church leaders said that the program would need to be adapted to the rural setting. There was no point in giving people flowers, because everyone had more than enough of them in their own gardens. So far, so good. But it was interesting what they chose to replace the flowers with—postcards with devotional thoughts. You can probably imagine something like this: "God so loved the world..." printed over a sunset, a rainbow, or an apple tree. I had a slight suspicion that they were not quite sticking to the second rule of the program.

Then, the church members went out to do the exercise. Half an hour later, they gathered in the church. Each person was asked to report on what had happened. The first person began, "Well, I handed over the card, then we stood there in silence ... and stood ... and stood ... and then I closed with Scripture reading and prayer." The second person said, "I greeted them with the Scripture for the day and then said a word of prayer." The third person had read Psalm 23. And so it went, on and on and on. When it was the pastor's wife's turn, she said, "I just sat down and listened. That time was so important for both of us." If I remember correctly, she was the only person who had kept to the rules.

## Why is it that so many people who enter the church through the front door leave it through the back door before long?

I found this evening rather typical. Although I can whole-heartedly rejoice with groups like this one who don't find it difficult to quote the Bible to people, I cannot avoid the sneaking suspicion that "Scripture reading and prayer" have become the default interaction style of people who have forgotten how to visit others *just for the fun of it*.

Please don't misunderstand me. I have nothing against Scripture reading and prayer. However, I believe that a church has lost something important if every activity is evaluated in terms of how often the Bible is quoted. In fact, there are strong indications that the evangelistic attractiveness of a church would be greater if there were more activities that happened *just for the fun of it*.

### Why people leave the church

Some time ago, I read an interview in a Christian magazine of a young man who had recently been converted and was reflecting on his former life. "You know," he said, "the only thing I still miss is the fellowship I used to have with the guys down at the tavern. We used to sit around, laugh, drink a pitcher of beer, tell stories and let our hair down. I haven't found fellowship like that with Christians. I no longer have a place where I can admit my faults and talk about my struggles without receiving a sermon, a frown and being quoted a Bible verse."

Such statements are depressing. Is that one of the reasons why so many people who become Christians soon turn their backs on the church? A survey conducted by Charles Arn revealed that Christians who remain in the church for a long period of time have an average of seven friendships within the church, whereas people who leave the church after an initial "decision" have an average of only two friendships at church.

Charles Arn's conclusion: The "friendship factor" seems to be at least as important for spiritual growth as are the theological factors.

If a church exclusively offers meetings that emphasize evangelism or Christian doctrine, their efforts can easily backfire. Many of the people who enter such a church through the front door as a result of this strategy leave it through the back door before long. Churches that emphasize evangelism should not be afraid to hold meetings that are designed exclusively to deepen friendships between Christians and give them opportunities to make new friends.

> In any friendship a relationship has developed whose primary purpose is simply to enjoy one another.

### Meetings that are just for the fun of it

Organize meetings in your church that are just for the fun of it. Go sightseeing together. Look for ways to help each other. Invite church members into your home. Have meals together. Take time to work with someone on a hobby. In any true friendship, a relationship has developed whose primary purpose is simply to enjoy one another. Christians who have forgotten how to do this are poorly equipped to win the world for Jesus Christ.

In some churches the leaders are always asking, "What will be the spiritual outcome of this meeting?" Time and again I have experienced that it is a great relief for these churches to be allowed to get together for no other purpose than just to be together. After one church I was working with had carried out a *Just for the fun of it* activity—they called it a "festival of love"—one member asked, "Why don't we have more activities like this?" Yes indeed, why not?

## A group experiment:

- *As a group, carry out an activity that is similar to the "spring greeting" described above. Adapt it to your situation—but make sure to stick to the rules! Afterwards share how you felt the activity went and what you experienced. Have fun!*

# Exercise 3:
# "Boredom forbidden"

I have read more than 200 books on the subject of love, both by Christian and non-Christian authors. Almost every author at some point addresses the question of what is the opposite of love. Generally speaking, there are two primary answers that are given. One set of authors suggests that "hatred" is the opposite of love, whereas the other suggests that it is "fear."

I believe that both answers express a truth about love, but I would like to suggest a third possibility. It seems to me that the opposite of love is *boredom.* By this, I don't mean to imply that every church that is not boring is automatically loving. However, a loving church will never be boring. Love releases so much creativity that there is no room for boredom, indifference, and apathy.

There is no doubt that love, as we find it in the Bible, will be marked by tolerance. We have already mentioned this. However, I am convinced that there is one thing we should not tolerate—boredom in the church.

If boredom is the opposite of love, tolerating boredom means tolerating the absence of love. And in this specific area, I believe that most of us are already far too tolerant.

### "It's so terribly boring..."

Perhaps you shy away from using the word—but isn't it true that a lot of the church meetings you've been to are just plain boring? If you haven't experienced meetings like that, so much the better. But when you are in a boring meeting, ask yourself whether it might perhaps be due to a lack of creativity in love.

> A loving church will never be boring. Love releases so much creativity that there is no room for boredom, indifference, and apathy.

I once asked a young member of a cell group what she thought was the greatest problem with the group. She answered, "It's so terribly boring!" Again and again I hear of boring churches or church groups. Nothing new ever happens. Everything is routine. And people who are bored are likely to bore others. Thus the vicious circle of boredom never ends.

### Back to our first love

The problem of fading enthusiasm occurred in the early church, too. It is probable that God had just such a situation in mind when he gave John the following message for the church in Ephesus: "I know your deeds, your hard work and your perseverance ... Yet I hold this against you: you have forsaken your first love. Remember the height from which you have fallen" (Rev. 2:2-5).

The first love is a love that burns with passion. People who have just come to know Jesus usually display this kind of love until time passes and they begin to fall into a negative, fault-finding, skeptical attitude (often under the influence of "more mature" Christians). At some point they begin feeling bored, and then they begin to bore others as well.

The problem is that hardly anyone recognizes this boredom as a spiritual problem: an indication of the absence of love.

How can we return to our first love? The text in John's Revelation continues, "Repent and do the things you did at first. If you do not repent, I will come to you and remove your lampstand from its place" (Rev. 2:5). The way back to our first love is the way back to God himself. To the degree that we encounter him—in all three dimensions as described in this book—we will be able to reflect his passionate love in our own lives.

## Four characteristics of holistic small groups

If routine and boredom are indicative of a spiritual problem, we cannot expect to solve it by some methodological gimmicks, such as decorating our meeting room with balloons or hiring a professional entertainer. Rather, we should address the root of the problem. In *Natural Church Development,* I speak about the crucial role of what we call "holistic small groups." Ideally, every church member should be part of such a group. What are the most important characteristics of this kind of small group?

*1. Holistic small groups are challenging.*

Each group meeting challenges the participants to greater spiritual growth. In holistic small groups, Christians don't waste time in artificial conversations about questions that nobody is asking ("Are the wings of the angels made out of plastic or wood?"). Instead, they continuously learn new things in order to apply them in daily life. They experience how the body of Christ really works, with each member sharing his or her particular spiritual gifts for the benefit of the whole group. Being a part of such a group is really exciting!

> In holistic small groups, Christians don't waste time in artificial conversations. Instead, they experience how the body of Christ really works.

There are groups that act like spiritual firefighters (and are deliberately designed to fulfill this purpose). When a small flame of enthusiasm breaks out, they quickly extinguish it. Holistic small groups do just the opposite. The members act as bellows, making sure that the fire of enthusiasm burns with an ever brighter flame, and kindling the flame anew in believers whose fire is burning low or has been completely extinguished.

*2. Holistic small groups involve the whole person.*

In holistic small groups people live out their faith in community. Each member feels free to share his or her questions and concerns with the rest of the group. Their interest in one another extends beyond the group meetings as well. Holistic small groups are an excellent training ground for growth in love. Because of the positive, safe relationships they share, they can keep an eye on one another and, if necessary, correct each other.

Holistic small groups, according to the terminology introduced in this book, integrate all three colors of love: justice (green), truth (red), and grace (blue). Though these groups may never have thought about it in these terms, what they are actually doing is living it. Their sessions are focused on the head, the heart, and the hands at the same time.

*3. Holistic small groups are need-oriented.*

Since individual Christians have different needs, there should be different kinds of groups within a church. The more variety there is, the greater the possibility that each person will find a group that responds to his or her needs. It is a pity that many churches have only one type of group, and that this type is often regarded as being the only type: singing, praying, Bible study, singing, praying, finish. How boring!

> We should make sure that the fire of enthusiasm burns with a bright flame, so that it can be kindled in believers whose fire is burning low.

One important characteristic of holistic small groups is that they are able to see beyond the needs of their members to the problems of individuals outside the group. Holistic small groups try to provide solutions for the needs in their communities—shopping for a mother who is ill, driving elderly people to the doctor, looking after children, etc.

*4. Holistic small groups multiply.*

Since they are a place where Christian love is put into practice, holistic small groups are highly magnetic. It is only natural that new people will join the group over time. However, no group can grow endlessly without losing its character as a holistic small group, which usually takes place when the group reaches a size of about twelve members. Many groups don't do anything at this point—and discover that growth naturally comes to a halt. The group therefore remains small and personal—how nice!—but it is unable to reach a greater number of people with the love of God.

Holistic small groups are deliberately built on the principle of multiplication: two groups become four, four become eight, and so on. Thus, it is possible for individual groups to remain manageable and personal, but it is also possible for a growing number of people to experience the love of God in the context of a small group. The real fruit of an apple tree is not an apple, but another apple tree. Likewise, the real fruit of a Christian group is not a new Christian, but a new Christian group.

# A group experiment:

• *As a group, discuss the four characteristics of holistic small groups mentioned above. Ask yourselves the following question: Which point seems to be the weakest in your group life? After identifying a specific weakness, invite each member to come to the next meeting prepared to share one suggestion for improving in this area. Give each member ten minutes to present his or her solution—and, if possible, put it into practice immediately.*

**Chapter 4:
Growing together**

# Exercise 4:
# "Glad you're here"

A few years ago, I participated in developing a "welcome packet" that would be given to first-time visitors of a specific church. Being aware of the fact that first-time visitors are completely overlooked in many churches, I thought this "welcome packet" was an excellent idea and invested a lot of thought in it.

I would have loved to have been able to simply state the real message of the packet on the title page: "We love you." In some parts of the world, I have been greeted with precisely these words as I have entered a church, and I liked it. However, in the cultural setting of the church I was helping, to have literally said "We love you" to a total stranger, would probably have made them think, "What space ship did you just get off?" What other words could we use to communicate the same message?

> By saying "We're glad you're here!" we show our appreciation for the fact that the other person is living on this planet.

**How do we say "I love you"?**

We finally decided to print the following words on the title page: "We're glad you're here." I was very pleased with this culturally appropriate way of saying "We love you." When we use expressions like this, we show our appreciation for the fact that the other person is living on this planet. We show our joy about his or her very existence. We communicate, "I'm glad you're the person you are—and not just because of the function you fulfill." These words, while being wonderfully tender expressions, can still be spoken to a stranger without fearing that he will be scared away.

We should cultivate the spiritual discipline of "noticing" in our churches. Tell another person what you like about him or her. Thank someone who has done something well. Every word of praise and thanks that passes your lips contributes to an atmosphere of love in your church, and that is what will make your church attractive. There are churches in which such words are never—and I mean *never*—spoken. Sometimes people even argue that Christians don't need that sort of motivation, since they are doing "everything for the Lord." You know what? The very Christians who say such nonsense are the first people who should train themselves to speak words of appreciation and praise.

**A helpful exercise**

In a seminar on church development in Lucerne, Switzerland, I decided to try an experiment. The seminar participants were divided into groups of no more than seven people. Each group member was asked to share in a few words what they thought was honorable, beautiful, or positive about each of the other group members. There was only one condition for this exercise: Everyone had to be honest.

Though I was the one who had suggested this exercise, I had left it up to one of the church leaders to assign each participant to a specific group.

Before I knew it, I found myself in a group with six people that I hardly knew. I immediately realized how awkward the situation was. All of them would of course expect me, the seminar leader and the "expert," to demonstrate how to find positive words for people, on the spur of the moment. And I had no clue what I would say!

The other group members each took a turn. Each of them told me what they liked about me. What a massage for my emotions! I was experiencing firsthand how pleasant such an exercise could be. But then it was my turn. I looked into the eyes of each of these wonderful people who had showered me with compliments, and was overwhelmed with such love that it was not difficult to find positive words for every single one of them. I had observed throughout my lectures that one participant was constantly smiling at me. Is it possible he had sensed how dependent I am on such expressions of appreciation while speaking? I told him so. Then there was a woman wearing the strangest pair of earrings I had ever seen. If I had been visually assaulted by those earrings in a store window, I would probably have thought them dreadful, but on her ears they looked glamorous. I told her so. And then there was the pastor who seemed to be trying to get on my nerves all day with his sarcastic humor. How I love people like him! I told him so.

### There is so much to say!

After everyone had said something positive, we all shared our surprise at how many things could be said, even to a virtual stranger. One lady, who had immigrated to Switzerland from El Salvador a few years earlier, told me the following after the seminar, "In Latin America it is perfectly normal to pay people such compliments. Since I have been living in Switzerland, I have progressively lost the habit. When we were doing the exercise, it reminded me of the warm-hearted atmosphere of my former home." It would probably be good for all of us to experience a little more Latin American warmth in our churches.

Tell each group member one thing you appreciate about that person.

## A group experiment:

• *Over the course of the coming week, each group member should send a postcard to every other group member naming one thing he or she appreciates about that person (please don't send e-mails, only postcards!). To facilitate this exercise, pass out previously addressed cards at your group meeting. Only positive things should be written—but remember to be honest. At your next meeting, share how easy or difficult you found it to make—and to accept—these compliments.*

# Exercise 5: "Let me walk in your moccasins"

On an Indian reservation in the United States, I found the following saying posted on one of the houses: "Until I have walked in my neighbor's moccasins for two weeks, I will not accuse or judge him." It seems to me that this would be a good practice for every Christian to adopt. It is a valuable exercise to put ourselves in the shoes of the people we relate to and try to see the world through their eyes (see pages 87-90).

Some people believe they are acting out of love by relying completely on their own feelings. But that can be a big mistake. Sure, there are some people who can intuitively sense the wishes and needs of others, but it is not always like that. I have heard of countless situations where this has provoked one relational belly flop after another. They have the best of intentions and a "heart overflowing with love"—but they consistently stick their foot in their mouth. They're clueless as to why people around them react so strangely to their overflowing expressions of love. After all, they meant well. But they surely failed to practice the art of walking in their neighbor's moccasins.

### The rules of fishing

I have the impression that most churches find it extremely difficult to apply the moccasin principle, especially when it comes to evangelism. Many Christians insist, at least in practice, that it is more important for the bait to be tasty to the fisherman than to the fish. Sometimes the situation is even more absurd: Christians demand that the bait has to be tasty to the fisherman's friend—the pastor, a denominational leader, an influential church member—someone who already knows Christ and doesn't need to be evangelized, yet is allowed to choose the bait. "Love demands that we take them into consideration," we are told.

> Until I have walked in my neighbor's moccasins for two weeks, I will not accuse or judge him.

Whenever I hear things like this, I am so glad that we have integrated "truth" into our three-color paradigm. That enables me to shout loudly, "No! No! No!", and to see my criticism as a genuine expression of love. Love does not demand that we take the fisherman's friend into consideration. Rather, it demands that we meet the needs of those we hope to win—and not allow ourselves to be hindered by our fellow Christians. We should never let the term "love" to justify the self-centered attitudes of other believers.

I enjoy fishing very much, even if I am not very successful at it. If my personal tastes (I have a distinct preference for Mexican food) as a fisherman were the standard for choosing bait, I would definitely choose to put a warm tortilla with an extra helping of salsa and guacamole on the hook. That would perfectly suit my taste, as well as the taste of my friends who share my enthusiasm for Mexican food. All of us would be very happy in this endeavor. There's just one tiny problem. We probably wouldn't catch a single fish. I really don't know why (and I find it difficult to understand), but fish seem to have a strange preference for slimy worms. If one of my friends were to come to me and say, "You really ought to use different bait. Worms are disgusting," you would hardly think me unloving if I replied, "But they're not for *you* to eat. I want to catch fish."

## Homemade problems

Many churches still need to come to grips with this simple logic. Whenever Christians begin to tread creative new paths in order to win people for Christ, you can bet your boots that it will be other Christians who give them the most resistance. *They* don't like the bait, so they demand that a different bait be used, one *they* are familiar with.

**Many Christians insist that it is more important for the bait to be tasty to the fisherman than to the fish.**

We consistently break the first and most important rule of communication: Consider how the message we send will be heard by those who receive it. In other words, we have not yet walked in our neighbor's moccasins.

## "A Jew to the Jews..."

Nobody has expressed this principle more clearly than the apostle Paul. His life was a practical illustration of how the moccasins principle works in everyday life. "To the Jews I became like a Jew, to win the Jews. To those under the law I became like one under the law (though I myself am not under the law), so as to win those under the law. To those not having the law I became like one not having the law (though I am not free from God's law but am under Christ's law), so as to win those not having the law. To the weak I became weak, to win the weak. I have become all things to all men so that by all possible means I might save some" (1 Cor. 9:20-22).

That means that when we plan our evangelistic efforts, we must think in terms of the needs of our target audience, rather than fixing our eyes on the methods that *we* are accustomed to. When we begin new groups, the questions and concerns of those we hope to win should be determinative, as opposed to the norms *we* have established in our groups up to now. When we plan a worship service, the taste of those attending must be the most important criteria—not the cultural or stylistic preferences of those who are in charge of the service.

In short, we must find out the needs and expectations of our target group. That sort of analysis has nothing to do with being manipulative. It is quite the opposite. It is a test of how serious we are about love. The decisive factor is how the message will be received, not what it was meant to communicate.

# A group experiment:

• *This section describes the importance of "wearing your neighbor's moccasins" in relation to people who are outside the church. However, in order to train this principle, it is relatively unimportant whose "moccasins" we practice walking in. They could just as well be the moccasins of a fellow Christian who has radically different views.*

**The decisive factor is how the message will be received, not what it was meant to communicate.**

*Find out which issues have divergent opinions among the members of your group. Then choose two members who will represent the different opinions (e.g. "A" believes that peace can only be secured by force of arms, "B" advocates a position of radical pacifism).*

*In the conversation that follows, A will defend B's position, and B will defend A's position. Afterwards discuss how you felt during this role-play exercise. In some of my seminars I have even seen some people radically change their opinions due to this exercise—merely because they have put themselves in the other person's shoes (for the first time!).*

*Possible conflict situations for this role-play exercise:*

*Christian vs. non-Christian*

*Parents vs. children*

*Traditionalist vs. reformer*

*Non-political Christian vs. political activist*

*Risk-taker vs. cautious personality*

*Conservative vs. liberal*

*Leader vs. church member*

*Established group member vs. new member*

*Rich church member vs. poor church member*

# Exercise 6: "The oikos principle"

There is no deed more loving than helping other people come to know Jesus Christ personally. We usually call this "evangelism." Some Christians, however, get a knot in their stomach just by hearing this term. It is not because they don't want as many people as possible to encounter the love of God, but simply because they have found a number of evangelistic methods so embarrassing or personally threatening that they have sworn to themselves, "Never again!" Will this exercise, then, be an attempt to motivate people to go and stand on the street, telling total strangers about the gospel and handing out tracts?

There are Christians for whom that sort of activity is just up their alley. They have a special gift for sharing the Gospel with anything that moves—and as a result they lead many people to faith in Jesus Christ. These are Christians to whom God has given the gift of evangelism. All they are doing is being faithful stewards of that gift.

### Not everyone has the gift of evangelism

Most Christians, however—exactly 90% according to our surveys—don't have this gift. I am among that 90%, as are 90% of my readers. What, then, can we contribute to the task of reaching the world for Christ? Can we do no more than stand at a distance, looking on in admiration or indignation, silently praying that things don't get too embarrassing? No, there is an alternative. Everyone who has *not* been given the gift of evangelism—and it is perfectly normal that most Christians don't have this gift—should discover the *oikos* principle. Let me tell you what it is all about.

> It has always pleased God to spread the good news through oikos relationships.

In order to find out how most people actually come to faith (in reality, not in theory!), we surveyed 1,600 Christians. Each person was asked to check all the factors that had contributed to their making a personal decision for Christ. Among the factors listed in the questionnaire were the following: "pastor," "visitation program," "evangelistic meeting," "friends/relatives", and many more. Do you know what the result of this survey was? An overwhelming majority of committed Christians—76 percent—can trace their "spiritual roots" to friends or relatives who brought them to Christ and the church. Only 5% checked "evangelistic meetings"; 4%, "visitation program"; and less than 0.5% came to faith through media, such as Christian radio or television.

### What the oikos principle is all about

That is the point of the *oikos* principle. "Oikos" is the Greek term used in the New Testament for "house," and in both the Greek and Roman cultures the term "house" not only referred to the immediate family, but also included the servants, the servants' families, friends, and work colleagues. *Oikos* stood for the whole sphere of a person's influence, his or her network of social relationships. It has always pleased God to spread the good news by means of *oikos* relationships. There is no evangelistic method on planet earth that is more effective.

Why is the *oikos* principle so powerful? I believe that the greatest reason is that only in a relationship is it possible to demonstrate the effect that genuine Christian love has on our whole lives. On radio or television we can only *talk* about love, but in an *oikos* relationship it can be experienced first hand. Any group that has grown in love and is beginning to spread the aroma of love can make amazing discoveries when applying this principle. The whole approach basically consists of two pillars—the "extended family" and the "potential congregation."

### The extended family

Rather than investing great effort trying to connect with people we do not know, the *oikos* approach suggests that we first concentrate on the contacts we already have, which is usually already more than we can effectively deal with. Your "extended family" includes everyone within your sphere of influence who does not yet know Christ and with whom you have a trusting relationship. How large is this group? Take some time to make a list of your relatives, friends and colleagues and ask yourself which of these people do not yet know Christ.

> Ask 100, 200 or 500 people what they expect from a Christian church. Then it should be clear what you have to do.

The diagram on page 133 suggests different areas of your life where you may know non-Christians (note that the church can also be such a place, for instance, when it comes to visitors). As you think through these areas of your life, pay special attention to those who, for whatever reasons, might be most responsive to an encounter with the love of God. Begin to pray for those individuals every day. That is enough for starters. You can be sure that this in itself will set off a dynamic process.

### The potential congregation

Your potential congregation is the total number of people in the extended families of the individual church members. One of our surveys showed that, on average, each Christian has nine close contacts with non-Christian friends, relatives, or colleagues. Following these statistics, a church of 100 members would have a potential congregation of 900 people. If we assume that about 300 of these contacts "overlap," we can still identify 600 individuals who are sure to be among the most receptive people in your area. You are already in touch with their needs, their problems, and, above all, you have the most efficient resources to reach these people with the love of God—Christians who have a trusting relationship with them. The concept of the potential congregation is aimed at extending the inward-focused ministries of the church to the needs of its potential members.

How can you be certain you truly understand the needs of these people? There is a surprisingly simple method. Ask 100, 200 or 500 people within your potential congregation what they expect from a Christian church. Then it should be clear what you have to do.

# A group experiment:

• *Using the diagram at the bottom of the page, each group member should identify the people in his or her "extended family." Remember that your "extended family" includes everyone (a) with whom you have a good, trusting relationship and (b) who does not yet know Christ. After you have filled in this diagram, tell the other group members the names of one to three people you wish to focus on in the coming weeks and months. Tell the group something about each person, and about the type and intensity of your relationship with them.*

*Throughout the coming weeks, spend at least ten minutes in each meeting sharing the progress and difficulties you are experiencing in reaching them with the love of God. Pray consistently and very specifically as a group for the extended families of the group's members.*

On radio or television we can only talk about love, but in an oikos relationship it can be experienced firsthand.

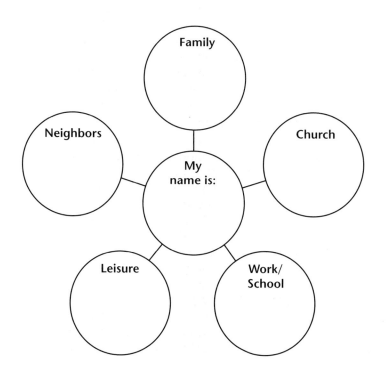

Family

Neighbors

Church

My
name is:

Leisure

Work/
School

**Chapter 4:**
**Growing together**

# Exercise 7:
# "What are your gifts?"

E veryone who knows me has discovered that I rarely miss an opportunity to explain the concept of spiritual gifts to my fellow-believers. Gift-oriented ministry is one of the most powerful instruments that God has given us for our lives as Christians and for the development of his church.

## The secret of gift-oriented ministry

What is the secret behind this concept? Gift-oriented ministry takes seriously the biblical teaching that the church is the body of Christ. Every Christian is a unique member of this body, and therefore has a specific role to play. Your part depends on the spiritual gifts that God has given you. That is why you need to know what your gifts are.

> *Every Christian is a specific part of the body. Your part depends on the spiritual gifts that God has given you.*

In our research we have discovered that 80% of all Christians have no idea what their spiritual gifts are. However, the Bible clearly teaches that every believer has at least one spiritual gift (1 Cor. 12:7-11; 1 Peter 4:10). If you don't know what your gifts are, it is not because you don't have any, but simply because you haven't discovered them yet. At the same time, once you discover your spiritual gifts, you will discover what God has called you to be.

## Olli, the ex-rocker

To illustrate this principle, let me introduce you to my friend Olli, whose picture you see on page 135. Olli is a 350-pound ex-rocker. Some time ago, Jesus appeared to him in a prison cell and he gave his life to Christ. Since then he has devoted himself to spreading the love of God to people on the edge of society: prostitutes, junkies, dropouts. When Olli turns up in red light districts and starts to talk with people, you can be sure that it won't be long until there is another shout of joy resounding in heaven because another sinner has repented.

Olli is one of those rare individuals who can speak about Jesus with anything that moves. He has an extremely well-developed gift of evangelism. But he also has other gifts: mercy, deliverance, healing, and—to the horror of some—the gift of leadership. At least those were the results when Olli did our *Three-Color Gift Test,* which is included in my book, *The 3 Colors of Ministry.* At first I had a hard time believing the results of our own test, because I thought of leadership as being rather different from what I saw in Olli. So I asked him if he thought he really had the gift of leadership.

"Christian, when are you gonna get it into that birdbrain of yours," he said in his unique mixture of local dialect and his own private grammar, "A leader's the one all the little chicks go waddling after. And they all come waddling after me!"

I could only agree. Indeed, a leader is someone people follow. On a number of occasions I have waddled after Olli, and each time I have benefitted greatly. He is a wonderful leader, and his gift of leadership is especially suited to those living on the margin of society.

You see, that is how gift-oriented ministry works, and that is how the body of Christ works. God calls someone like Olli and other Christians go waddling after him. I'm not an Olli, nor are you. That is fine. God has given each of us different gifts, and he doesn't want us to try to become clones of Olli. He wants us to live according to *our own* giftedness.

Anyone who understands gift-oriented ministry knows that there is no reason to be envious of anyone else's gifts, because each Christian has been given a different, unique gift mix. I don't have either the gift of evangelism or the gift of leadership, which makes me all the more grateful that God has given those gifts to others. Since they have them, I don't need to have them. Instead, I can focus on putting my own spiritual gifts into practice, and, to be honest, that still leaves me with more than enough work to do.

For example, God has given me the gift of teaching. I really enjoy sitting at my computer week after week and developing books such as *The 3 Colors of Ministry* or *The 3 Colors of Love* (and if God should decide to give me a long life, many more "3 Colors of..." books will follow). For someone with a completely different gift mix, like Olli, sitting in front of a computer screen writing new books would be torture. But for me that's exactly my cup of tea, and I know that God is using me precisely in this way.

Olli and I have frequently led seminars together. You can imagine the great fun it is for all of the participants, since the two of us fit together so well!

### Why gift-oriented ministry improves our ability to love

What do spiritual gifts have to do with the ability of a church to grow in love? A great deal! There are at least four reasons why gift-oriented ministry goes hand-in-hand with loving relationships.

*1. It helps Christians experience greater joy.*

Some people believe that suffering in their Christian ministry earns them a "perks plus" admission ticket to heaven. To be sure, there is genuine suffering for the sake of Christ in today's world. But it is my experience that many Christians are suffering simply because they are not fulfilling the task that corresponds to their God-given gifts. I am convinced that God is not a bit impressed by *that sort* of suffering. When we begin to live according to our gifting, three closely related

When Olli turns up in red light districts, it won't be long until there is a shout of joy resounding in heaven because another sinner has repented.

effects take place. First, we begin to enjoy our work far more; second, our ministry becomes considerably more effective; and third, we discover that God really does use us to build up his church. I have heard a number of Christians express that this threefold effect has been the deepest, happiest, most fulfilling experience they have ever had.

*2. It doesn't use people as a means to an end.*

One of the most painful experiences we can have is discovering that we are not loved for who we are, but because someone wants to use us to achieve a particular goal. This is a real danger in churches that don't operate on the principle of gift-oriented ministry. These churches are continually on the lookout for workers who can fill the empty slots in the ministry. When certain tasks need doing, "volunteers" are found to fill the gap (without considering their spiritual gifts). If no volunteers come forward, either a little "gentle" pressure is applied or a general appeal to people's guilty conscience is made.

**Whenever you discover that you don't have a particular gift, you have a reason to celebrate.**

This is not how the church was designed to function. When planning the church's programs, the leadership should begin with the gifts that God has given its members. It really doesn't matter if some jobs remain unfilled. Churches that dare to apply this principle radically usually report that, after a certain time, they are able to carry out significantly *more* ministries than ever before. They aren't necessarily the ministries they used to believe had to be done. But they are definitely those that God has created them to do.

*3. It delivers us from the myth of having to be a "jack of all trades."*

When I began to discover my own spiritual gifts, the first thing I discovered was a rather long list of gifts that God had *not* given me. At first, I was disappointed. But the more I thought about it, the more I realized that whenever I discover that I don't have a gift, I have a reason to celebrate. God, in his love, is revealing to me another area that should not be my ministry emphasis, unless what I am seeking is the gift of frustration!

Once I was asked to write an article about spiritual gifts for a Christian magazine, and I included this statement: "Whenever you discover that you don't have a particular gift, you have a reason to celebrate." Some weeks later, when I was sent a copy of the magazine, I looked in vain for this wonderful sentence. The editor had changed it, obviously believing that it was a misprint, into, "Whenever you discover that you don't have a particular gift, it's no reason to give up." But I hadn't meant "no reason to give up." I truly meant "a reason to celebrate!"

Celebrating means uncorking the champagne (or, depending on your convictions, at least a bottle of lemonade), dancing, and singing songs of praise! Obviously, the well-meaning editor of the magazine had not been able to imagine what a deep, liberating, spiritual experience it can be to discover that God has *not* given us a certain gift—and therefore does not expect us to become frustrated trying to use it.

Applying the principle of gift-oriented ministry means that you are not expected to have all the abilities and to do everything. Dare to be one-sided! Concentrate on using your spiritual gifts and don't let anyone give you a guilty conscience for not fulfilling tasks that you were never meant to fulfill.

*4. It helps you identify your true identity.*

When you have found your spiritual gifts and live according to them, you discover your true identity as a Christian. In many of the roles you fill, you can be replaced, but no one can replace you in your role of being you. Churches that take gift-oriented ministry seriously are able to help people find and develop their God-given uniqueness. They encourage them to become strong, creative, distinctive individuals.

Perhaps the nature of love is that I gently and lovingly lead you back to yourself.

### Everybody is an original

One of the most beautiful definitions of love I have come across in my research was phrased by Antoine de Saint-Exupéry. He wrote, "Perhaps the nature of love is that I gently and lovingly lead you back to yourself." Isn't that wonderful? If I love you, my aim will be to help you become what you already are in the eyes of God, and to come alongside you in certain areas of your life. Love does not try to mold the other person to fit my ideas. People are at their best when they are liberated to be who God created them to be.

My value as a person lies in the fact that I am the person God intended me to be. The same applies to you. There are people who would prefer to measure everyone with the same yardstick. They would like all Christians to be the same. If we gave into this tendency, we would soon be out of unique personalities; no joy, no creativity—and nobody to waddle after Olli.

# A group experiment:

• *Spend one—or better, several—group sessions discussing how to discover and use your spiritual gifts. As your working material for these sessions you may want to use the book "The 3 Colors of Ministry," which includes, among other things, an extensive gift-discovery questionnaire.*

# Exercise 8:
# "May I pray for you?"

Recently, I heard the following report about a weekly prayer group in Argentina. The group has developed the custom of sending several of its members to visit two households in their neighborhood before each meeting. What they say is simply this, "Our prayer group is meeting in half an hour. Do you have any special needs we could pray for?"

When the group comes together, the requests mentioned by the people they have visited are shared and brought before God in prayer. One week later, the visits are repeated. This time, they say, "We prayed for you a week ago. Have you noticed any changes?"

> Every Christian ought to be able to know that at least one person at church prays for him or her regularly.

### Caring enough to pray

The members of the prayer group reported that, in several cases, they had experienced noticeable answers to their prayers. Can you imagine what an impact that had? The people they had visited learned: "There is a living God who is concerned about me!" And even in those cases where no visible change could be observed, the people being prayed for had learned something important. Now they knew, "There is a group of Christians in the neighborhood that is interested enough in us to ask about our concerns and pray for them."

Having heard about this group, I was not surprised to learn later on that several people had become interested in the gospel as a result of this activity, and some had even become Christians. This prayer ministry is a wonderful example of the close link between prayer, love, and church growth.

### Prayer and the ability to love

In his book *Peace Within Marriage,* Karl Mandel quotes some interesting statistics. He writes that in the United States one out of every two marriages ends in divorce. But here is a more interesting fact: "Of all married couples that pray together every day, only one marriage in 1,105 ends in divorce." That really isn't so surprising, is it?

Prayer is a particularly valuable means of expressing our love for other people. We should be ashamed that there are so many church-goers who are unaware of anyone in their church who prays for them regularly. Those churches usually don't have a high love quotient, either. Every Christian ought to be able to know that at least one person at church prays for him or her regularly. Some churches have set up prayer chains for this purpose; others have created special prayer services; others place a special emphasis on prayer in their small groups. Creativity that is inspired by love can find countless possibilities. But we need to really do it.

If we remember what actually happens in prayer, it is no longer surprising to us that prayer and love are so closely linked together. When

I pray for someone, I expect God's love to flow through me to that person. That reality is particularly well expressed when you pray for someone while laying your hands on him or her. Perhaps that kind of prayer is the best way to experience how the love God has given us actually touches other people.

### The healing power of love

Medical research shows that love can physically and mentally heal. I believe that God included this principle in creation in order to reflect his nature. Therefore, I simply don't understand why people play down such cases with comments such as, "It's not really a miracle when a person is healed as a result of the love he or she received in the church. It's purely a psychosomatic phenomenon." Is it only considered a miracle if someone is healed without love, in a context of hatred, fear, or boredom? It is a strange image of God that lies behind such a notion.

God acts in such a way that his love—we also could say, his Spirit—flows through us to other people. The Bible says, "God has poured out his love into our hearts by the Holy Spirit, whom he has given us" (Rom. 5:5). This can happen through prayer, and it can also happen through the whole range of possibilities presented in this book. Each of these can become a channel used by God to reach out to his creatures with his supernatural love.

> When I pray for someone, I expect God's love to flow through me to that person.

I have often come across Christians who have argued passionately—and sometimes with great aggressiveness—about whether a certain act of healing was brought about by the Holy Spirit or by love.

Can somebody please tell me what the difference is?

## A group experiment:

• *As a group, carry out the prayer exercise that was described at the beginning of this section. Afterwards, share your experiences and evaluate the results. Consider whether you might want to do this kind of prayer ministry on a regular basis.*

**Epilogue**

# The greatest power on planet earth

A number of years ago, I wrote to some public figures in Germany, asking them what they thought was the most significant thing each of us could do to bring about peace. I received many good answers. The German Chancellor, Helmut Kohl, wrote that it is most important "to think beyond your own interests, to be prepared to understand other people's problems." The conservative politician Franz Josef Strauss emphasized that "however radical and hard the controversy" it is important that we only have "opponents," never "enemies." Erhard Eppler, at that time a leading spokesman of the socialist party, wrote that we should strive for dialogue "with those who would be our opponents in case of war."

But the best of all answers came from Pastor Johannes Busch, the leader of *Bethel Center,* the largest European institution for the mentally and physically handicapped. "We cannot do anything for peace," he wrote, "unless someone else has first given us peace and helped us to overcome hate and enmity. The most important thing each of us can do for peace is to open ourselves to receive love." Among the weighty statements of the politicians, this response from a Christian pastor almost seemed a bit naive. Could that really be the answer to the serious problems of the world?

### The proof of real life

I am convinced that this is, in fact, the solution. It agrees with the teaching of Jesus. People often give the impression that Christian love is unrealistic and impractical. It might be something for solemn sermons and sentimental Christmas messages, but in real life, in politics, in situations of racial or religious conflict, it definitely has no place. But is this really so? In this book, I have used the examples of Martin Luther King, Francis Schaeffer, and Mother Teresa as real-life illustrations of individuals who sought to put Christian love—in fact, very different aspects of Christian love—into practice. You may or may not like these people. You might be able to identify hundreds of weak points and personal failures in their lives. But even the harshest critic has to admit that each of them has had an immense impact. The world has literally been changed because of the legacies that these people have left. They have shown me and millions of others that the message of Christian love is not just something suitable for printing in golden letters on Christmas postcards, but that it can well pass the test of real life, in the midst of conflict, hatred, suffering, and terror.

> The most important thing each of us can do for peace is to open ourselves to receive love.

### Can we really live this?

Some years ago, I wrote the lyrics for a musical about Martin Luther King, hoping to help spread his message—loving your enemies, nonviolence, and the vision of social justice—to people who would be unlikely to read theological or political books. I can well remember how the composer of the music, Siegfried Fietz, almost choked on some of the words when he tried to sing them for the first time. The words of one song are as follows:

"Take away our wives and attack our children—and we will still continue to love you." Siegfried stopped singing and said, "I cannot sing this. I'm not that far in my life yet. Can anybody live up to that standard?"

### The redeeming power of love

I told him that these words were taken from an actual experience in which Martin Luther King had to prove that he was really prepared to live out the message of loving his enemies. Some of his opponents had carried out a bomb attack on his house. He heard about it while he was speaking at a mass meeting. He brought the event to a close and hurried home to see if his wife and child, who was only a few months old, were injured. When he arrived, an agitated crowd had already gathered around the house. The situation was tense. People were singing, but they were angry and horrified. Many of them had weapons in their hands.

Unarmed love is the strongest weapon on planet earth.

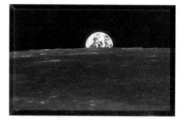

Martin Luther King stepped out onto the shattered veranda. "In some ways, it was the most important hour of his life," his wife Coretta said later. "His own house had just been bombed, his wife and baby could have been killed; this was the first deep test of his Christian principles and his theories of nonviolence." Grave and calm, he stood before the crowd and raised his hand. They quieted down. He spoke in a soft voice, "I want you to go home and put down your weapons. We cannot solve this problem through retaliatory violence. We must meet violence with nonviolence. Remember the words of Jesus: 'He who lives by the sword will perish by the sword.' We must love our white brothers, no matter what they do to us. Jesus still cries out across the centuries, 'Love your enemies.' We must meet hate with love." Coretta King relates, "Many people in the crowd were crying. I could see the shine of tears on their faces, in the strong lights." But most importantly, the crowd put away their weapons and dispersed. A white policeman said, "If it hadn't been for the black preacher, we'd all be dead."

### Stronger than all the armies in the world

We should never forget that Martin Luther King's message of nonviolence and love for our enemies was successful. Former enemies, in fact, became friends. Prejudices and hatred, in many instances, disappeared. When Siegfried recorded our songs in Atlanta with Coretta King, she told him, "Martin firmly believed that unarmed love is the strongest weapon on earth, that love liberates with a redeeming power. And I hope that all who loved and admired him will join us, so that his dream will one day come true."

If we strive to grow in love, we are not indulging in a private pleasure for Christian dreamers and idealists. Christian love is the strongest force on planet earth. People who open up themselves to this love, practice it, and share it with others, can have a far stronger impact on the course of history than all the armies in the world.

One of the greatest privileges in my life is to serve alongside our network of NCD National Partners in about 60 countries, among them countries that are centers of political, racial, and religious conflict. In the context of this ministry, I have encountered innumerable examples of how churches have applied the principles of Christian love—sometimes in a markedly hostile surrounding—and experienced how both they and their non-Christian surroundings are being transformed, step by step. Can you imagine what might happen if they continue in this vein? If these processes are intensified? If they multiply? I can. The outcome will definitely be a different world.

> The secret is that love is a force that bears within itself the power to create more love. It multiplies to the degree that we share it.

### How love multiplies

The secret is that love is a force that bears within itself the power to create more love. It multiplies to the degree that we share it. A simple mathematical calculation reveals the startling results this could have. If this year just one person found one other person, and together they learned to share Christian love, and if both of them in the next year found one more person to pass this love on to, and if this process repeated itself year after year, after about 32 years, half the world's population would be reached—and after 33 years, love would have reached the whole world.

Perhaps you feel that this goal is too lofty. But what is to stop us from setting this goal for our own churches? If just a few Christians were to start practicing the art of love—growing in justice, truth, and grace—surely they could set a similar multiplication process in motion.

### The revolution is not yet complete

A key experience for me was my visit to Uwe Holmer, the pastor who had taken the communist dictator Erich Honecker into his home after the revolutionary events in Eastern Germany. Uwe Holmer emphasized strongly that, although the Berlin Wall had come down, it made him sad that only a few people were able to practice something radically new. Contempt, discrimination, hatred, narrow-mindedness, a Berlin Wall running through our heads and hearts, even Christian heads and hearts—that is our true problem. And it is a worldwide problem. "It really hurts me," Uwe Holmer told me, "that all of this takes place in the name of a new way of thinking and in the name of a peaceful revolution." And in a quiet voice he added, "The revolution is not yet complete. It is my deep desire that it come to completion by the revolution of the love of Christ."

It is my prayer that you will experience how fulfilling it can be to be used by God to help bring about this revolution.

# NCD Implementation Resources: The "how to" series

NCD
tools

**NCD Implementation Resources** are designed to strategically help you get the most out of Natural Church Development in different spheres of church life. Look for the following titles that relate to *The 3 Colors of Love*:

- ## How to Implement
  ### The 3 Colors of Love
  ## in Your Church

  Dozens of worksheets, checklists, and implementation ideas for pastors and church leaders. Includes a CD-ROM with all of the diagrams of *The 3 Colors of Love* for use in teaching, as well as software to help you analyze the composite *Fruit of the Spirit* results of individual small groups or your whole church.

- ## How to Study
  ### The 3 Colors of Love
  ## in Your Small Group

  Enables small group leaders to guide their groups through the life-transforming process of growing in love. Provides suggestions for one, three, six, or twelve sessions.

- ## How to Use
  ### The 3 Colors of Love
  ## in a Mentoring Relationship

  A tool developed especially for one-on-one discipleship processes. Designed to start a powerful multiplication process that doesn't depend on money, marketing, or big conferences.

**ChurchSmart Resources**
3830 Ohio Ave., St. Charles, IL 60174, USA
Phone: 1-800-253-4276
E-mail: orders@churchsmart.com

NCD
tools

# NCD Discipleship Resources: The "3-Color" series

**NCD Discipleship Resources** are designed to be practical tools for each of the eight quality characteristics of Natural Church Development. Here are the titles that have been published or are in process:

- ### The 3 Colors of Leadership
  (for the quality characteristic "Empowering leadership")

- ### The 3 Colors of Ministry
  (for the quality characteristic "Gift-oriented ministry")

- ### The 3 Colors of Spirituality
  (for the quality characteristic "Passionate spirituality")

- ### The 3 Colors of Life
  (for the quality characteristic "Functional structures")

- ### The 3 Colors of Worship
  (for the quality characteristic "Inspiring worship service")

- ### The 3 Colors of Community
  (for the quality characteristic "Holistic small groups")

- ### The 3 Colors of Evangelism
  (for the quality characteristic "Need-oriented evangelism")

- ### The 3 Colors of Love
  (for the quality characteristic "Loving relationships")

# Natural Church Development: A different approach ... for different results